Cambridge Elements ≡

Elements in Publishing and Book Culture
edited by
Samantha Rayner
University College London
Leah Tether
University of Bristol

IS THIS A BOOK?

Angus Phillips
Oxford Brookes University

Miha Kovač
University of Ljubljana

CAMBRIDGE
UNIVERSITY PRESS

CAMBRIDGE
UNIVERSITY PRESS

University Printing House, Cambridge CB2 8BS, United Kingdom

One Liberty Plaza, 20th Floor, New York, NY 10006, USA

477 Williamstown Road, Port Melbourne, VIC 3207, Australia

314–321, 3rd Floor, Plot 3, Splendor Forum, Jasola District Centre,
New Delhi – 110025, India

103 Penang Road, #05–06/07, Visioncrest Commercial, Singapore 238467

Cambridge University Press is part of the University of Cambridge.

It furthers the University's mission by disseminating knowledge in the pursuit of
education, learning, and research at the highest international levels of excellence.

www.cambridge.org
Information on this title: www.cambridge.org/9781108940344
DOI: 10.1017/9781108938389

© Angus Phillips and Miha Kovač 2022

First published 2022

A catalogue record for this publication is available from the British Library.

ISBN 978-1-108-94034-4 Paperback
ISSN 2514-8524 (online)
ISSN 2514-8516 (print)

Additional resources for this publication at www.cambridge.org/isthisabook

Is This a Book?

Elements in Publishing and Book Culture

DOI: 10.1017/9781108938389
First published online: May 2022

Angus Phillips
Oxford Brookes University

Miha Kovač
University of Ljubljana

Author for correspondence: Angus Phillips, angus.phillips@brookes.ac.uk

ABSTRACT: This is a book about the book. Is this a book? is a question of wide appeal and interest. With the arrival of e-books, digital narratives, and audiobooks, the time is right for a fresh discussion of what is a book. Older definitions that rely solely on print no longer work, and as the boundaries of the book have been broken down, this volume offers a fresh and lively discussion of the form and purpose of the book. How does the audiobook fit into the book family? How is the role of reading changing in the light of digital developments? Does the book still deserve a privileged place in society? The authors present a dynamic model of the book and how it lives on in today's competitive media environment.

KEYWORDS: book, publishing, audio, business model, reading

ISBNs: 9781108940344 (PB), 9781108938389 (OC)
ISSNs: 2514-8524 (online), 2514-8516 (print)

Contents

Introduction: The Three-Body Problem

Way back in the previous century, on a clear summer night in the early 1970s, a young hitchhiker was resting in a field near Innsbruck in Austria, gazing at the stars and dreaming of galactic travel. An idea formed in his head and a few years later Douglas Adams submitted a draft to the BBC for a radio play entitled *The Hitch Hiker's Guide to the Galaxy* (HG2G). BBC Radio 4 broadcast the first episode on 8 March 1978, followed by one episode a week until 12 April (the final two episodes were written with John Lloyd). Due to its success, in the next two decades followed another radio series, a vinyl album, a TV series, a computer game, comic books, a film, and the trilogy of novels (in five parts) that were also published as audiobooks. Adams reworked the narrative each time the story went through a media transformation so that in the end there are almost as many versions of the story as there are formats in which it appeared.

In the 1970s and 1980s the ability to access the range of HG2G products was limited by geographic and temporal constraints and by the accessibility of the media in which the content appeared. To listen to the radio show or TV series, one had to live in the UK and tune in at a specific time and day when the series aired. To play the video game, one had to own the video game console and have access to a store where games were sold. Similarly, HG2G vinyl albums and books were sold in the UK, the USA, and Canada and in some better-stocked stores in continental Europe – and that was it.

One of the authors of this book, who back then lived quite close to the field where Douglas Adams was looking at the stars that night (just on the other side of the Alps, on the Communist side of the then European divide), happened to find the first book in the HG2G series in the early 1980s whilst browsing in a bookshop in Camden Town in London. He found himself there by coincidence when he was hitchhiking around Europe for the summer holidays, spending nights in parks and cheap hostels, and ended up in London because he got a lift there. For the majority of book readers, such a chance encounter in a bookstore was the only way to access and find interesting books.

Fifty years later Douglas Adams would be called a multiformat story-teller or cross-media author. As in a science fiction novel, all the media of his life – cinema, television, radio, LP, cassette, book, typewriter, computer, CD-ROM, and comic – were miraculously squeezed into a device smaller than a paperback called a smartphone. This made all his works, in a wide variety of formats and categories, accessible to any smartphone user with internet access. The co-author of this study, who over time has lost his penchant for both sleeping in parks and hitchhiking, repurchased the five-volume trilogy in digital format and accessed its audio and video derivatives via smartphone from the comfort of his armchair, exactly 1,554 kilometres away from the bookshop where he bought the printed version of the book in the early 1980s (and of course he calculated the distance with his smartphone). From his perspective at least, in the past half-century this represents a radical cultural and social change comparable to the fall of the Berlin Wall.

What has happened to the book as a medium in these rapidly changing times? How has digital technology changed the formats, production, and perception of the book? Does the book still have the same social, cultural, and educational function as it did in analogue times? What role does reading play in understanding the media properties of the book? How has the social role of the book and the meaning of book reading changed in the age of digital screens and media convergence? All these questions are difficult to answer because, as we will show, there has never been a clear idea of what a book is and what it does. As Rüdiger Wischenbart noted in 2008, the UNESCO description of the book (see Chapter 3), which held dominance in our understanding of what a book is, did not 'bother to say much about the originator or the industry that produced the book, nor its realm, distribution or economy; nor does the definition discuss the book's audience or the process of reading' (2008, 197). In short, it was a simple description of an object without looking at the complexities of the book's existence.

With all this in mind we co-authored two papers with Adriaan van der Weel and Rüdiger Wischenbart on the importance of book statistics for media and reading research (2017) and on what a book is (2019). The first paper outlined the measurable properties of book production and consumption. In a second step it analysed the reasons such statistics are necessary. In a third step it proposed the measurement tools that would make the current ecosystem of book reading and publishing more transparent and comprehensible. The second paper was a natural extension of the first; whilst looking at the gaps in contemporary book publishing and reading statistics, it struck us that more new formats and forms of what we call the book had emerged in the previous two decades than in the preceding century. From this arose the need for a new definition of the book; after all, how could one produce book statistics without clearly defining the main object of measurement?

The 2019 paper did not provide a final and clear-cut answer to this question. The present book is a continuation, dealing with those questions that were only briefly touched on in the two papers, such as the concept of the book as it exists in book history and the role of publishing business models and reading in understanding what a book is and what it does. In doing so we have answered some previously mentioned unanswered questions but – as is the case with any interesting research – we have also opened up a few new ones.

We should state that we take a primarily Western-centric approach to our discussion of the book. A longer work would consider perspectives from other parts of the world, including China, where printing started, or Brazil, where innovative audio recordings of literary works were produced from the 1950s to the 1970s.

In the first chapter we look at the many forms of books that exist in today's book markets and show the social and cultural reasons behind defining a book. In the second chapter we consider controversies in the description of the book as they have arisen in book history. We challenge the approach that counts as part of the book family every piece of written or printed text that was produced, from cuneiform to digital books. We consider such an ecumenical approach misleading, especially if it is based on the assumption that all these physically distinct artefacts that existed in different eras and cultures served similar social and cultural functions. As we will show, in book history debates these common, transhistorical functions have never been described in detail but instead employed vague terms such as 'aura of the book' and 'bookishness'. On this basis we concluded that the book as a concept had become a blind spot, a floating signifier in publishing studies and book history.

In the third chapter we show that the printed book achieved special status in the media landscape of Western societies, triggering the need for a technical definition of the book. Here we build on the 2019 paper 'What Is a Book?' and show that the physical properties of the printed book as they developed over the past three centuries gave rise to a book information architecture. We follow this line of reasoning and consider a book not as a thing but as an information architecture that can have a variety of manifestations.

In the fourth chapter we pay special attention to the audiobook as an outlier in the book family. This provides the starting point for understanding the role of book information architecture, the differences between an audiobook, podcast, and audio first series, and the role of reading in the debate over what constitutes a book.

In Chapter 5 we analyse the special status of the printed book in the production and framing of knowledge and information in Western civilization. The book as a medium also framed us as individuals since our perceptions and our ways of thinking were influenced by the object we were observing; our perspective was both inside and outside the object of our research. Following the line of reasoning developed in Adriaan van der Weel's *Changing Our Textual Minds*, we call this social and cultural conjuncture the Order of the Book. We build on van der Weel's work by detailing further the protocols and rules that emerged as the consequences of a culture 'whose entire social fabric is defined by the textual codes of manuscript and print' (van der Weel, 2011, 91).

In the sixth chapter we outline different modes of reading and discuss both how long-form linear reading relates to the Order of the Book and how the role of reading is changing in the digital landscape. Next, in Chapter 7 we discuss the business model of the book, relying on a set of intermediaries between the author and consumer. Throughout history this business model – similar to Robert Darnton's communication circuit of the book – had two main forms, a payment model and a membership/subscription model, where the subscription – very often in the form of library fees – was based on the user's payments or on public money. This model survives into the digital age, albeit with a smaller number of intermediaries and with algorithms as new intermediary players in the field.

All this leads us to the conclusion that the book has three main characteristics that form its social, cultural, and media identity: (a) book-specific information architecture, (b) a set of properties that made possible the Order of the Book, and (c) a business model. These three interrelated parts form something akin to the Three-Body Problem in physics: an open, unstable system for which there is no general solution in closed form. This creates a difficulty: it is impossible to create a unique and long-lasting definition of the book. There are conjectures put forward in which the 'three bodies of the book' form the impression of a stable system, as in the UNESCO definition of the book. However, such stability is only temporary, existing only in the eye of the beholder, who often projects it on to other positions of the three parts or even on to media circumstances in which one of these three parts does not exist. Closer analysis shows that in some cases, with each change of position, the nature of each part also changes. This opens up a whole new debate about what a book is and what it does, which we hint at in the Conclusion.

1 The Variety of Books

In the 2020s for most people the book still means the printed book. It is familiar as an object and has shown great resilience in the face of competition from other media and attempts at the book's reinvention in digital form. Comparison with digital content has led to a renewed emphasis on the production quality of printed books, as publishers see the value for readers of the design, paper, and illustrations. The book in digital form has been the subject of much experimentation, but what is striking is that the most commercially successful format is the vanilla e-book, mirroring the structure (architecture) of the printed book. This type of digital book works well for fast-paced, linear narratives such as genre fiction. Catching up fast is the audiobook, a growing area of publishing. Meanwhile whole categories of publishing have migrated to the Internet, from reference to travel.

What are the types of book today? We commonly associate the book with text-based fiction and narrative non-fiction, and e-books are widely accepted by readers. There are other examples of products that would meet a traditional definition of the book – being printed volumes with a certain number of pages – from colouring books to silent picture books for children. Yet with little or no text, do they still qualify as books? With regard to the audiobook, we pay close attention in later chapters.

The Book in Print

If those set on burning books were going to get to work, would they choose an e-book or a CD-ROM? No, they would head to the nearest library or book-shop to source some printed material. Clearing someone's Kindle does not make a strong enough statement. The printed book remains the most visible and central form of the book. During the pandemic of 2020 bookshelves became the backdrop to many a Zoom call. The former prime minister of the UK, David Cameron, was spotted ensuring he had the right backdrop for an interview: 'Politicians take care over their choice of background. David Cameron caused a ripple while promoting his own book, when a spot-the-difference game over two separate photo shoots pointed up that he'd removed a Hitler biography (big, black font on the spine) from his shelves. Did he worry that we might think he was a fan rather than a reader?' (Heathcote, 2020).

The printed book is also a reliable technology. The printed text benefits from the economies of scale available from the printing press, and its boundaries are set by the production system. To keep their prices competitive, and due to printing technology, books have constraints around length, the number of illustrations, and the optimum format. The traditional response of publishers to falling or static sales is to publish more titles. This is encouraged in turn by falling print costs and by the growth of digital printing, which facilitates ever smaller print runs and the printing of single copies to meet individual orders (Clark and Phillips, 2019).

A physical product can be owned and passed round friends and family; in the digital era it became a refuge from screens for office workers or parents seeking amusement for their children. Giving a physical book as a present says something about the recipient and also about the giver. The book in print confers status and symbolic capital:

> The symbolic meaning of the book imbues its readers with a certain affective and social status. Even a sense of identity might be said to attach to books; hence the persistence of the old saw 'show me your book case, and I will tell you who you are'. What is important in all these cases is the *visibility* of books, resulting from their materiality, and the obvious ownership relation projected by this visibility'. (van der Weel, 2010, 54)

Russian oligarchs may never open a book but still want to fill their libraries with leather-bound volumes. Country hotels need a book-lined lounge in which guests can relax. Chic cafes play vinyl records and use books to decorate the walls.

Yet the book is off-putting to some who are daunted by a visit to a bookshop or the thought of opening a book. The 2020 Booker Prize winner Douglas Stuart, the author of *Shuggie Bain*, said of his upbringing: 'As someone writing a working class story – as a boy I always felt excluded by books' (BBC, 2020). In 2018 the UK retail chain WHSmith, which sells a range of goods from stationery to books, was voted the country's worst retailer on the high street. The retailer was criticized for its poor customer service and out-of-date look. Authors leapt to its defence, arguing that it reached book buyers other shops could not reach and that some buyers see more traditional bookshops as intimidating. The writer Joanne Harris said: 'While it may not be the coolest shop on the High Street, research suggests that WH Smith, and not Waterstones, is the place where most working-class people buy books' (Cernik, 2018).

In his 1979 poem 'A Martian Sends a Postcard Home', Craig Raine called print books Caxtons, 'mechanical birds with many wings' (Raine, 1979). Printed books come in many formats and production values, from pocket editions to luxury collector editions. Leah Price proclaims the variety of print 'across historical periods and even within a single culture. They come in different sizes and shapes (a hefty coffee-table book vs. a dainty pocket diary), are bound to their owners for different periods of time (a family Bible passed down from generation to generation or a textbook loaned to another student for the year), invite or at least allow different uses (reading or wrapping)' (Price, 2019, 29). That variety in print is now enhanced by experimentation with digital technology to transform the book.

The Digital Book

Books have been presented on CD-ROM, as apps, and as enhanced e-books with multimedia. The high costs of such projects, against relatively low sales and low retail prices, have so far proved largely unsustainable in consumer markets. However, in educational and academic markets, digital content and services have replaced many print products (Clark and Phillips, 2019).

In the 1990s, when the digital book began to be developed commercially, the view was that in this new format the book could take off in many directions. The use of hyperlinks would enable books to connect to a host of external content, from text and image archives to live video streams. Instead of embedding a video file in the e-book, hypertext links would be added to the text. Jack Schofield wrote: 'books are fixed, finite things contained between covers. The electronic online book is different: it is kinetic, distributed, constantly changing, almost alive ... an online book can not only refer to things outside itself, it can enable the reader to link to them without leaving the book' (1994). Of course the Internet itself now offers this functionality and much reference and other content has shifted online.

In turn books continue their promise of permanence and internal consistency, preferring not to send readers off at tangents (Phillips, 2014).

There has been playful reworking of the structure of the book in digital formats. Books can easily be produced along the lines of Create Your Own Adventure, with multiple routes through a story. The risk is that this is the territory of gaming, and most narratives benefit from being presented in a straightforward, linear format. Some books like educational textbooks are not often read from beginning to end – discrete chapters will be accessed – but for fiction and narrative non-fiction, linearity remains of great benefit (Phillips, 2014). Liza Daly confirms that 'text adventures weren't the future of novels, CD-ROMs weren't the future of non-fiction, and . . . the meteoric rise of ebooks hasn't been accompanied by a flowering of interactive experimentation from traditional authors and publishers. But quietly, games have been filling that gap' (Daly, 2013).

The inclusion of multimedia in the book should offer exciting opportunities. A notable success in the market was the release of the Solar System app in 2011 by Faber and TouchPress. Steve Jobs used the product to demonstrate the iPad 2 at its launch. Highly interactive, offering the ability to rotate planets with your finger, the product won an award for the best app of 2011. The app was born digital, created for the market opening up around the iPad. Yet the app was described as a book: 'A breakthrough electronic book about the Solar System, offering hours of interactive exploration and presenting a treasure trove of visual information . . . This much-anticipated new title from Touch Press . . . raises the bar yet again on what an electronic book can be' (apps.apple.com). By that Christmas Faber was releasing the print book of the app, written by Marcus Chown, who provided the text for the digital edition. Overall, however, book publishers have struggled to make the app business model work, with a large number of failures amongst born digital projects. From the days of CD-ROMs through to apps, multimedia projects have subsumed large budgets whilst the market has required low prices to attract buyers. Book apps have to compete in a crowded space (2 million apps are available to download on the Apple Store) and have achieved little impact. Book publishers have mostly abandoned the publishing of apps.

Reference is a category of publishing that has suffered in the face of online competition, ranging from Wikipedia to a multitude of user-generated content. Arguments in the pub are quickly settled by consulting our mobile phones. Yet there remains a market for authoritative reference works. The second edition of *The Oxford English Dictionary* (1989) is still available in print: in twenty volumes the reference work traces the usage of words through 2.4 million quotations from a wide range of international English language sources. The CD-ROM version appeared in 1992 but was discontinued in 2017 since it would not work on new operating systems. Most users today will access the online edition, which is regularly updated. In September 2020, 650 new words, senses, and subentries were added, including 'code red', 'craftivist', and 'Cookie Monster'. Consulting the dictionary for its definition of a book reveals two relevant entries: firstly, 'A portable volume consisting of a series of written, printed, or illustrated pages bound together for ease of reading'; secondly, 'A written composition long enough to fill one or more such volumes' (*Oxford English Dictionary*). The print edition is certainly a book, but is the online edition a book or a database? Website copy refers to it as an online publication. Users access it using the search function, with little sense of the A to Z arrangement of the print dictionary.

Consulting *The Oxford Companion to the Book*, edited by Michael Suarez and H. R. Woudhuysen, suggests that a book can appear comfortably in both forms, print and digital. Their own volume is a book 'in the abstract, non-corporeal sense (and can thus be described in its Internet manifestation), and also in the physical sense of a three-dimensional object in codex format' (2010, 543). Their book appeared in print as well as part of the Oxford Reference online resource. But what if an online text does not appear in print simultaneously? We do not regard Wikipedia as a book, nor do we see a blog as a book. What of a novel that appears solely online and has not been published as an e-book or in print – is that a book? Writers contributing to literature sites such as Wattpad are certainly writing stories long enough to be published in book format, but when do those become a book? Does a book require an act of publication in a book-specific business model or the transformation of the text into the architecture of the book? We will deal with these issues in more detail in Chapter 3.

The most successful digital transformation so far has been the vanilla e-book (Phillips, 2014), reproducing the look of the printed page. For enthusiastic readers of genre fiction, e-books offer great value with low prices on individual titles and available subscription services. Dedicated e-readers are also free from the distractions present when reading on your phone, laptop, or tablet: 'Because they are standalone devices that don't ring or beep (like phones) or let us toggle elsewhere (like tablets), they may turn out to be more like print' (Baron, 2015, 149). The e-book offers extra functionality compared to the printed book – for example, search (an index is no longer required) and the ability to adjust the type size – but it also possesses disadvantages such as little sense for the reader of their progression through the text. Many readers of print have a clear map of the book in their head and can quickly find an earlier passage, looking on the left or right page, with an idea of how far they were in the book. As three meta studies have shown, especially when reading longer texts with informational content, readers in print remember more than those who read the same content on screens (Singer and Alexander, 2017; Delgado et al., 2018; Clinton, 2019). Print books retain their symbolic value for both authors and readers, allowing the expression of identity and ownership; whilst Adriaan van der Weel argues that 'it seems doubtful that ebook reading confers any more symbolic capital than digital reading at large' (van der Weel, 2014, 45).

Advocates of the container theory of books argue that books are ripe for disaggregation in digital form. Brian O'Leary said, 'We need to think about containers as an option, not the starting point. Further, we must start to open up access, making it possible for readers to discover and consume our content within and across digital realms' (O'Leary, 2010). This happens in academic markets where readers may encounter chapters in large databases alongside journal articles. The publisher adds an abstract and a list of keywords and the chapter starts to become a single unit separated from the original volume. Readers browsing the text may not realize its ancestry as part of a whole book. In 2006 Kevin Kelly, the co-founder of *Wired* magazine, argued for a universal digital library in which books cease to be 'isolated items, independent from one another'. Links and tags would be added to connect books together so that the library becomes one very large, single text.

> At the same time, once digitized, books can be unravelled into
> single pages or be reduced further, into snippets of pages.
> These snippets will be remixed into reordered books and
> virtual bookshelves ... Once snippets, articles and pages of
> books become ubiquitous, shuffle-able and transferable, users
> will earn prestige and perhaps income for curating an excellent
> collection. (Kelly, 2006)

This approach faces first the hurdle of copyright and then the opposition of
authors and publishers keen to earn a return from publications. Additionally,
many authors (and their readers) would prefer their work to remain in
a unified whole rather than be cast adrift in a world of remix and mash-up.

Silent Books

Most books involve text but some books are silent, from children's picture
books to colouring books. A children's picture book can tell a story without
the need for any printed words – we still call it a book because of its physical
format, yet no reading is involved. Parents may describe the story to their
children, introducing their own narrative. Some books of course display an
artful mix of words and pictures, and as Lewis Carroll's Alice thought: 'what
is the use of a book ... without pictures or conversations?' (Carroll, 1865, 1).

There are genres of publishing where few words may be employed. Take
a photography book such as *Exposure* by Jane Bown (2009), which contains
her portraits of a range of famous people from Bette Davis to Samuel Beckett.
There is a one-page foreword by David Bailey and a four-page introduction.
There is no commentary on each portrait – simply a blank page opposite with
the name of the subject and the date the picture was taken. They are
wonderful pictures and little reading is required to enjoy the volume.

In the UK, in 2013, a book appeared titled *Everything I Know about
Teaching*, with the author given as Michael Gove, the then secretary of state
for education. In 2021 it was still on sale at £4.99. Apart from the chapter titles,
each page was entirely blank with ruled lines enabling the book to be used as
a notebook. The selling copy offered: 'Over 90 blank pages of Gove's teaching
wisdom – the perfect gift to put a smile on the face of any UK-based teacher.'

Similar titles include *Everything Men Know about Women*. Such books cannot be read and there is little story beyond the title, but they have the paratext of the book, such as a title, title page, and back cover blurb (Genette, 1997).

Colouring books benefit from the low tax regime of the book and also appear in the guise of the standard printed work. Although there is no author, there usually needs to be an illustrator to construct the lines. When the colouring book craze took off all over the world in the first decade of the new millennium, it was put down to a rise in craft activity and people looking to reduce anxiety and raise their level of mindfulness. Notable successes were *Secret Garden* and *Enchanted Forest* by Johanna Basford, which sold millions of copies worldwide: 'In 2011, the British publishing house Laurence King asked Johanna Basford, a Scottish artist and commercial illustrator specializing in hand-drawn black-and-white patterns for wine labels and perfume vials, to draw a children's colouring book. Basford suggested instead that she draw one for adults. For years, she told her publishers, her clients had loved to colour in her black-and-white patterns' (Raphel, 2015).

What about a desk diary? Those still using a paper journal have an object that is often sold as a book with an ISBN (more on the role of ISBNs in Chapter 3). It may have some printed content – for example, tables of time zones and weights and measures – but it is completed by the user and they become the author of the text. Diary entries from famous people may be converted into book form if of sufficient interest. The original diary, however, is surely in manuscript form although within a bound volume.

At Length

Does a book have to be a certain length? Traditional constraints around economics and technology suggested a minimum length in many categories and established printing methods work in multiples of signatures, or printed sections, most commonly of sixteen pages. A few decades ago a short book of 27,000 words, such as the present volume, would not command a decent price in the market and would feel insubstantial to readers. Yet led by shorter books in digital form, which in turn found a print market, shorter books in physical form have become widely accepted not only in academia but also in fiction publishing.

Short stories may be published individually in magazines, but to appear in a book they would traditionally be collected together. The story 'Cat Person' by Kristen Roupenian, about a bad date, first appeared in the *New Yorker* in 2017 and provoked an amazing reaction, going viral and being described as the most famous short story of the century. The story is still available to read online for free, and its success led to a book deal for its author. She published a collection of short stories in book form, *You Know You Want This*, in 2020. In the meantime *Cat Person*, a story of around 7,000 words, was published in print as a 72-page paperback (2018), with photographs, and as an e-book. One Amazon reviewer commented that 'It will take you longer to download it to your Kindle than it will to read it!' The volume had the appearance of a book but the publisher downplayed this aspect by proclaiming that Roupenian's first book was still forthcoming.

Beyond a certain page count books become unwieldy and are split into separate volumes. *The Oxford Companion to the Book* appears in two volumes of around 650 pages each. Surely the arrival of the digital book should have released the length constraints of the book. There is no reason why books cannot get longer and there is no need to break longer texts up into separate volumes. Reference works become part of databases, sold mainly to institutional clients. Yet e-books have the same commercial considerations as print, and if the author or publisher can develop and sell a series of shorter books, that makes keener financial sense.

Reading

Reading is of course not only book reading. As we will discuss in more detail in Chapter 6, reading is happening in many different ways through work, study, and social interactions. We read thousands of words each day – work and home emails, texts, social media posts, news bulletins – often at great speed. We have become expert at skimming for the key points and headlines across reports, articles, and web postings. This type of reading is functional, necessary to obtain information or to communicate for work. Naomi Baron comments that 'one of the major effects of digital screens is to shift the balance from continuous reading to reading on the prowl … The result? The meaning of "reading" increasingly becomes "finding information" – and often settling for the first thing that comes to hand rather than "contemplating and understanding"' (Baron, 2015, 39). As the amount of information available expands at a fast pace, we can only aim to scratch the surface with our own reading. It is probable that AI will undertake more of this kind of work – machines can work across vast amounts of information, reading books, reports, and articles. Already AI can summarize research papers in a few sentences and the potential is there for personalized summaries of the information relevant to a person's interests and work. Meanwhile AI is writing simple news stories and can write formulaic fiction – the program GPT-3 from the company OpenAI can generate a story when given an opening sentence. Yet, as we will show in the chapter on reading, higher levels of reading such as deep reading remain a human domain and one of the prerequisites for analytical thinking.

If a motive for defining the book is to help us better understand reading, then digital forms of the book offer an advantage. User data can track how much of an e-book is read – this is almost impossible to establish with print books. When it comes to books opened and completed, the most passionate readers of e-books open 77 per cent of their books and complete 60 per cent of their purchases. By contrast average readers of e-books open 60 per cent of their purchases and finish only 40 per cent of their books (Kobo, 2016). The data also support the hypothesis that reading on a dedicated device is a more immersive experience compared to reading through an app on a phone or tablet (Baron, 2015; Kobo, 2016). Readers of e-books spend three times as much time reading on a dedicated device compared to reading through an app, and the most passionate readers of e-books spend 50 per cent more time on the e-reader.

In summary, books as we know them today appear in many different manifestations and offer a range of different experiences, from reading stories to the craft activity of colouring. Yet the problems with finding a common denominator and defining what a book is did not first appear with digitization. In the following short chapter we turn to the past, to the field of book history, a scholarly discipline in which the question of what is a book emerges in varied historical and cultural contexts. To the delight of any researcher, this is where things get really complicated.

2 A Brief Digression into Book History

Book history takes an ecumenical approach to the definition, or, rather, the description of the book. As Simon Eliot and Jonathan Rose point out in the introduction to the *Blackwell Companion on the History of the Book*: 'Book history uses the word "book" in its widest sense, covering virtually any piece of written and printed text that has been multiplied, distributed, or in some way made public' (Eliot and Rose, 2007, 2). Consequently, a book historian is interested in 'graffiti on a wall in Pompeii as well as in a letter by Cicero ... in a catalogue of the Great Exhibition of 1851 as well as in a first edition of *David Copperfield*' (2). The *Companion* is edited accordingly: it offers a chronological survey of the forms and contents in various formats from the third millennium BC to the third millennium AD, taking into account scrolls and clay tablets as forms of the book. Such an approach makes the book one of the oldest objects in human history, which in the past five thousand years has moved 'from one material form to another and spread to almost all cultures and climes' (5).

Although primarily focused on the age of printing, the editors of *The Book: A Global History*, Michael F. Suarez and H. R. Woudhuysen, point out in their introduction that the volume 'seeks to delineate the history of the production, dissemination and reception of texts from the earliest pictograms of the mid-4th millennium to recent developments in electronic books' (Suarez and Woudhuysen, 2013, xi). In *The Concept of the Book*, Cynthia Johnson emphasizes that book history encompasses 'production, dissemination and the cultural impact of the book in myriad of forms (cuneiform, tablets, papyri, the parchment, codex, the printed and digital books)' (Johnston, 2019, 1). Likewise, Nicole Howard begins her survey of the book as technology 'with the generation of books that developed between antiquity (c. 800 BCE) and the European Renaissance of the fourteenth century' (Howard, 2005, 2). A comparable approach is taken by Frédéric Barbier in his *Histoire du Livre* (2001), by Martyn Lyons in *Books: A Living History* (2011), and last but not least by Zvonimir Kulundžić a few decades earlier in *Istorija knjige*, a canonical book history text in then socialist Yugoslavia (Kulundžić, 1959). The rationale for these multi-myriad forms of the book is summarized in the statement that the book 'performed similar tasks (they were read, bought, sold, collected ...), in different periods even if the physical form of early books was different from that of today's' (9) (see also https://en.wikipedia.org/wiki/Book).

Such a task-based understanding of the book was further developed by Germaine Warkentin in her short paper on Aboriginal sign systems in Canada. (1999) There she suggests that the concept of the book has to be defined functionally. 'The question cannot be, "What is a book?" but rather "How does a given culture define what a book *is*?"' (18) However, this does not mean that 'a book is whatever we want it to be . . . '; what makes a book to be a book, is what it does, that is, its functionalities in a given culture, which 'determines what it wishes to be its books' (19). Accordingly, some cultures exhibit 'bookishness', unifying 'the field of studies in the book from ancient times to the present day', but others cultures do not and 'have opted for other cultural objectives'. In her paper she showed how colliers (belts) fashioned with beads of wampum used by Mohawk Indians contained messages that conveyed complex information when performed by a skilled narrator and as such 'exhibited bookishness' (19). In Western culture, by contrast, the notion of bookishness allows us to distinguish 'blank forms and advertisements from the printing of books' (19) and, say, newspapers and airsickness bags from books. Warkentin avoids elaborating in detail on the concept of bookishness: she only hints that one of its main features might be the transmission of more complex information. The question of what is bookishness thus remains unanswered.

It should be mentioned that in the past decade, another meaning of the word *bookishness* emerged. Jessica Pressman uses the notion of bookishness to analyse a set of creative practices such as sculpture, film, design, and similar, that are focused on printed books. She thus employs the concept of book-ishness as a description of an aesthetic strategy that engages 'the physicality of the book within a digital culture, in modes that may be sentimental, fetishistic, radical' (Pressman 2021, 15). Yet, as with book historians, there is no detailed debate on what a printed book is and what has been its function in modern civilization that makes its uses in artistic practices look bookish.

Similarly undefined is the concept of the aura of the book. The most likely candidate for first coming up with this concept in media theory was Walter Benjamin in the 1930s, who used it to distinguish between auratic and non-auratic art forms: simply put, the former derive their aura from religious rituals. Embedded in a tradition and an established canon, they are considered unique and authentic. On the other hand, non-auratic objects are technically reproducible, thus substituting 'mass existence for unique existence'; they are 'detached from a sphere of tradition' and separated from their 'basis in cult' (Benjamin, 2008, 22, 28). For example, a statue of Venus in a Greek temple had auratic value in the Greek temple context but a photograph of the statue of Venus published in a book on Mediterranean archaeology has not. From this standpoint classical literary texts could be considered part of the canon and thus auratic, regardless of the fact that from the fifteenth century onwards they were technically reproducible and considered non-auratic (see Berret, 2017). In short, Benjamin's view of the role of the printed book appears contradictory because he failed to see the book as a technology. He saw only the textual content but remained blind to its physical incarnation in a technologically reproducible book format, thus making the notion of aura unclear and inconsistent. In turn Thomas R. Adams and Nicholas Barker (1993) speak of the cultural aura of books as artefacts without giving a specific meaning, and Simone Murray (2020) writes about '"radioactive aura" emanating from the book object itself' (43).

A broad and all-inclusive approach to the definition of the book, in combination with unclear notions such as 'aura of the book' and 'bookishness', raises further questions. For example, if book history encompasses 'virtually any piece of written and printed text that has been multiplied, distributed or in some way made public', would it not make more sense to speak of the history of printing, as suggested by Robert Darnton (1982), or the history of the transmission of texts, as suggested by Adriaan van der Weel (2011), rather than the history of the book? But if the history of the book is really the history of printing, how is it that newspapers or airsickness bags are never mistaken for a book? If the history of the book becomes the history of print, what remains as the objects of research for the history of the book? What makes cuneiform and the e-book members of the same family? With different materiality and born in different social and cultural circumstances, do they perform the same social and cultural functions as printed books? If yes, what are these common functions? If no, what makes these textual manifestations members of the same species? Why, for example, do we consider the clay tablet a predecessor of the book but not of the Excel spreadsheet?

Matters become more complicated if we bring reading into the equation. Cuneiform and wampum belts were most likely not read silently and critically – as, say, a student at a university in the American Midwest in the twentieth century read a book by Michel Foucault. Again this reading practice differed from that practised by monks in Europe in the fourteen century, or that of a present-day Wattpad user in South Korea, who is following a fanfiction story and perhaps writing their own instalments. An interesting historical and anthropological exercise would be to compare these reading practices, asking from which observation point they are all seen as bookish, and from which perspective radically different, and how the reading substrate correlates to different modes of reading.

Let us hypothesize that the blindness surrounding these dilemmas arises from the fact that book historians are by default educated through reading books. As Simone Murray puts it, 'because the book has been the default medium of information exchange, we have a tendency to look through it rather than at it' (Murray, 2020, 8); or in Van der Weel's words, 'paradoxically, the textual mediums are so central to human existence as to be largely invisible' (2011, 32): we do not see them because they 'frame our observations' and help to define 'who we are as human beings' (33).

This leads to the conclusion that the printed book has become something of a blind spot for book studies, as if a scholarly discipline could exist without defining its main object of research. In other words, in book history debates, the bookishness and the aura of the book became floating signifiers that point to no actual object and have no settled meaning. That is, we are discussing textual communication with a significant gap in the debate as we are not rigorous enough in defining the basic concepts with which we describe textual media – and this gap is predominantly the consequence of not being able to see the role of the observer's cultural mentality in the process of 'measurement' of what is the book, because their mentality is framed by the object of observation. When we try to understand information exchange in other cultures, eras, and civilizations by applying to them notions such as the book, aura of the book, and bookishness, we are projecting onto them traits of our own culture that we do not fully comprehend. We are not inclusively accepting all textual formats into the book family; rather we are simply exporting our blind spots to other cultures. Perhaps the blind spots can be better understood by looking at textual transmission in those cultures that invented printing and codex format independently of European civilization (for example in China), and by comparing developments in textual transmission across cultures with the use of more neutral concepts, away from bookishness and aura. Such an enterprise is beyond the scope of this little book and would require considerable interdisciplinary work.

Light can be shed on such conceptual issues by examining in more detail the social and cultural functions of the book as they existed in the West after the invention of printing. By taking such an approach we do run the risk of being accused of an overly Western-centric approach; on the contrary, we believe that some clarification of the conceptual muddle surrounding the notion of the book in our own place and time should be the first step 'to an understanding of how different formats of books may have never been forms of the same cultural object, recognizing that such a broad definition of the book was the result of our failure to analyse a specific social and cultural mentality that made us define a book in this way' (Kovač et al., 2019). As the social conjecture that gave birth to the notions of bookishness and aura originated in modern Western civilization (and not, for example, in China, which has its own, distinct history of printing), this is a natural starting point for such exploration. By creating a culturally specific description of a book and its functionalities, we go some way towards an answer to the question of whether the book can indeed be considered as a transcultural and transhistorical phenomenon, or whether we should use more neutral terms when talking about textual information tools and information transmission, storage, and retrieval in a global context and in different historical periods. In sum, a balanced debate is necessary, both about the development of textual media in different ages and cultures and about what books do in our own time.

In the following chapter we will start the discussion by looking at the material properties of the book after the invention of printing in the West and outline the changes in the technical definition of the book that have taken place in the past fifty years. In Chapter 4 we will discuss audiobooks as a special case and in Chapter 5 we will analyse in detail the rationale behind the special status of the book in contemporary society. This status necessitates a technical definition of the book.

3 Defining the Book

Searching for the common denominator amongst the many manifestations of the book, and experimenting with a definition of the book that would sum up all their main features in one or two sentences, would be considered an esoteric academic exercise were it not for the special status books have in many countries. As will be seen in Chapter 5, this special status gave birth to a set of book market regulatory mechanisms and other policies supporting the production and distribution of books. Without a technical definition of the book, these regulatory mechanisms could be applied to any printed or textual object that is arbitrarily declared to be a book, from an airsickness bag to a computer accounting program. There needs to be a clear rationale as to why the book deserves special status in comparison to other goods and services, for otherwise many book policies appear to be an arbitrary political invention favouring one industry over another and contradicting the rules of the market economy. Why should the book industry – and not the brewing industry – enjoy stimulatory measures such as lower value-added tax (VAT), fixed prices, and state subventions?

The legitimacy of interventions to help the book derives not from the physical properties of the printed book but from what a book does in a society by disseminating, framing, and storing predominantly textual content. The need for a technical definition of the book therefore results from how the book is viewed in contemporary society. If there is no consensus that society benefits from books, the regulatory mechanisms of the book market cannot be justified.

In other words, the societal definition of the book makes no sense without the technical one, and the technical definition of the book cannot be hardwired into regulatory mechanisms without elucidation of the social factors behind the book's special status. We examine the present technical definitions before turning to the societal and historical context in which a book becomes an object in need of protective policies.

A Technical Definition

In their volumes of *The History of the Book in the West*, Alexis Weedon, Jane Roberts, and Pamela Robinson see the millennium between 450 and

1450 as the era of the 'consolidation of the codex's position as the standard form for a book'. As Weedon stresses, the codex format with its 'list of contents, illustration, pagination, punctuation and indexes, which we recognise today as the printed book, did not suddenly appear in the mid-fifteenth century, it was a progressive development of many centuries' (2010, xi). By the second half of the twentieth century, some organizations attempted to define the book in its codex format in a clear-cut way (Kovač et al., 2019). In 1964, UNESCO defined the book as:

> a non-periodical printed publication of at least 49 pages, exclusive of the cover pages, published in the country and made available to the public.

A decade later, the United States Postal Service (USPS) defined the book as:

> a bound publication having 24 or more pages, at least 22 of which are printed and contain primary reading material, with advertising limited only to book announcements.

As Kovac et al. (2019) argue, the artistry of the USPS definition is 'that on the one hand it included illustrated books for children, with little text and fewer than 48 pages, and at the same time excluded commercial catalogues, newspapers and magazines containing advertising' (318). Yet a periodical without advertisements, such as a scientific journal, could also be considered a book. In 1971, this confusion was solved with the introduction of a separate identification number for periodical publications, the ISSN (International Standard Serial Number). A publication with an ISSN is not a book, even if physically it looks very much like one. The equivalent for books is the ISBN (International Standard Book Number).

For a brief moment in time, the problem of defining the book appeared to have been solved. Since all books made available to the public must have an ISBN (otherwise they cannot be sold and distributed to libraries and bookstores), it became possible to define a book as a publication that has an ISBN. Because the task of assigning ISBNs and ISSNs to publications was left to professionals such as publishers, book distributors, and librarians, there were few dilemmas surrounding the nature of published materials. Across the world ISBNs and ISSNs were assigned to all publications that met the UNESCO and USPS definitions.

Yet the waters were muddied with the arrival of digitization and devices such as laptops, tablets, and smartphones. Textual media such as books, newspapers, magazines, and journals migrated online. Digital objects have no physicality, but their appearance on the screen is often identical because 'the technology behind digital media does not frame them in the same way that print technology framed books, magazines, and papers' (Kovač et al., 2019, 318).

As long as the e-book was another form of publication of the printed book, this lack of framing did not present a new dilemma in terms of defining the book. When a title published in hardcover was issued as an e-book, it received a new ISBN in the same way a new ISBN was assigned to the paperback edition. But as stressed in the first chapter, e-books have developed their own ecosystem and many titles are published only in digital format, and some digitally with the option of print on demand. In an e-book ecosystem, there is little need for the boundaries as they exist in print (e.g. page extent with pagination) to form the backbone of the book's definition. Also a book can be published on Amazon without an ISBN. Digital encourages both aggregation and granularity (Cope and Phillips, 2006). As described in Chapter 1, educational and academic publishers began to sell e-textbooks and e-academic monographs by the chapter. The next step was to assign an ISBN to each chapter of the book, thereby seeing the part of a book as an equivalent to the whole: with this, the *differentio specifica* of the whole is lost. If we take this approach to its extreme, if each chapter is considered a book, then the totality of many chapters in many books should also be considered as a single book. Surely a library then becomes a book along the lines of the thinking of Kevin Kelly (discussed in Chapter 1). More complications arose when textual, book-length content (mostly fiction) began to appear on self-publishing platforms like Wattpad, but such texts are not seen as books. All the new forms of the book in the online realm place a question mark over its technical definition. Meanwhile print books still exist alongside digital content; as always, news of their death has been exaggerated (Kovač, 2015).

A possible solution to a technical definition of the book would be to consider the printed book as the core of a cluster of derivatives. These derivatives could be considered books as long as their content is organized along the principles of books. Here the concept of book information architecture provides a way forward. The idea that the book is an information architecture – not a product or thing – was elaborated by Cope and Phillips (2006, 8), who identified the main elements of the book's information architecture: title, cover, title page, author, linear structure supported by page numbers, chapters, and so forth, and body text sometimes supported by images. In subsequent debate and after much hesitation, long-form and immersive/deep reading were added alongside the elements of the book's information architecture (Kovač et al., 2019).

There were two reasons for the initial reluctance to include reading in the definition of a book. First, reading is something that happens in the reader and as such it is not an integral part of the physicality of the book; second, 'the categories of deep, immersive, and long-form reading are subjective and cannot be measured, defined, and standardized in a single way for each and every category of books and for each and every reader – at least not in a similarly exact way as UNESCO described the book through the frame of printing technology' (322). If reading is considered as one of the main properties of the book as a medium, we banish from the realm of books 'many objects that we are used to calling a book, such as audiobooks, silent books, colouring books, and gamified book-based story apps' (322). However, due to the fact that lower VAT, fixed prices, and other policies came into existence because of content that could be accessed primarily through reading, we decided to add reading to the definition of the book (more on the social role of reading in Chapter 6).

Books can therefore be viewed as content machines (Bhaskar, 2013) that primarily require reading and have their content organized according to book information architecture. Accordingly, a book can be technically identified through the following four criteria: a minimum length (24 pages as in the USPS definition), predominantly textual content, boundaries to its form, and content organized in a certain information architecture. Applying these criteria to the contemporary book ecosystem, a wide range of objects can be considered books, with the most book-like object being printed books, which meet all four criteria. The least book-like object is the colouring book, which has few elements of book architecture and no textual content (see Figure 1) (Kovač et al., 2019, 325).

For a long time, audiobooks sat comfortably and quietly alongside the world of print and they mostly fit the aforementioned description of the book. Matthew Rubery defines the audiobook as 'a single speaker's word-for-word recording of a book originally published in print' (2016, 3). This definition expresses the long history of the talking book and the close connections that remain between audio and print books: the vanilla

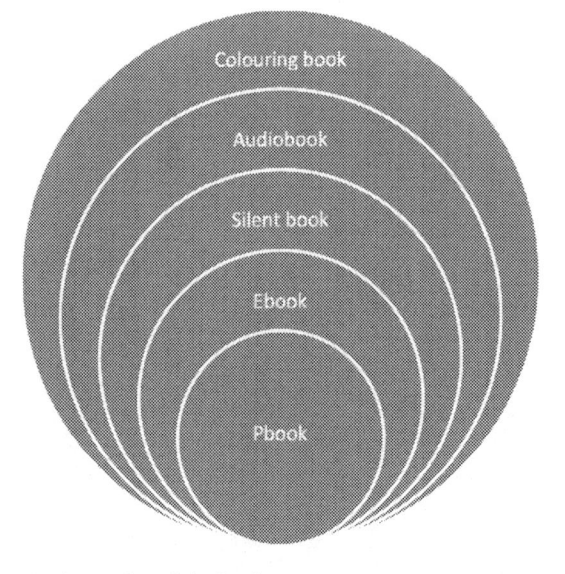

Figure 1 The hierarchy of the book

audiobook has been the most successful audiobook format. However, audio is now developing quickly on its own terms, with audio-first projects and the growth of podcasting, and some listeners may no longer make a direct connection between the audiobook and a print edition. We turn to the audiobook in the next chapter.

4 The Audiobook

One part of the book publishing industry that is seeing vibrant growth is the audiobook. For example, in Sweden audiobooks now outsell print books (57 per cent of the total volume of books sold in 2020) (Gustafsson, 2021), and in many countries the growth rate of audio is the highest of any sector of the industry. Audio is attracting new audiences and new projects are commissioned directly for this format, some moving beyond the single narrator with more theatrical performances.

Talking books began for people who found it difficult to read, from injured veterans of the First World War to those with a visual impairment. Mathew Rubery says that because of this 'recorded books became linked to disability in the popular imagination. Why listen to books if you can read them?' (Rubery, 2016, 185). By the 1980s, audio publishers were selling spoken word recordings to a much wider audience including commuters in their cars and busy people with little time for reading a printed book. Back then, critics regarded the audiobook as a threat to print – the same anxiety met the arrival of the e-book in the twenty-first century. Over time the medium of storage of the audiobook moved from gramophone disc to tape to cassette to CD – today wholly digital.

Why has the audiobook grown in prominence so quickly in the late 2010s and early 2020s? Like the e-book it is difficult to gift in digital format and yet unlike the e-book it has been around a long time – on LP, cassette, or CD (the last two formats ideal for a lending library audience). The reasons for the rapid growth of the audiobook market include technology and convenience, quality and breadth of content, and new audiences. Meanwhile some traditional print readers can see the attractions of audio as a way of bringing story into their busy lives.

Technology and Convenience

Audio has become very much part of city life. Travelling by public transport or walking around town, we can observe many people wearing earbuds; fancy headphones are no longer the realm simply of hi-fi buffs and have become desirable consumer items not only for listening to music but also for enjoying audiobooks and podcasts. Driving the listening trend is the ubiquity of smartphones that are always with us and can be bluetoothed to in-car and home speakers.

The possibilities for audio include synthetic speech offering automatically generated access to unlimited content. This was a feature on early Amazon Kindles and some users listen through programmes on their PC that convert text to speech. There have been skirmishes to ensure that audio rights are kept separate from e-book rights, and a robot voice cannot automatically read out the text without permission (Schofield, 2009). There is also the aesthetic question of whether listeners want a robotic voice: many recordings are sold on the brand of the narrator. Yet synthetic speech offers some advantages, such as a voice bespoke to the listener. Matthew Rubery comments:

> Audiences have grown increasingly sophisticated when it comes to judging the fit between narrator and script, especially in terms of sensitive issues like age, class, ethnicity, gender, nationality, race, and sexuality. To the discerning ear, there's no such thing as a neutral voice. Casting controversies might be averted, however, if synthetic speech technology were to give audiences a measure of control over the narrator's identity. Don't like a man reading to you? Swap him for a woman. The voice sounds too white? Switch to a Latino one. (Rubery, 2016, 275)

Quality and Breadth of Content

Demand for audiobooks is also driven by quality and range. Now digital, audiobooks are unabridged, free from the constraints of tape or disk. Data from the US market for 2020 showed that one in six books were sold in the digital audio format. The highest share was in adult non-fiction, and popular categories were business, self-help, and humour (Audio Publishers Association, 2021). There has been considerable investment in audio in recent years, from marketing spend to star narrators being signed up alongside a cadre of polished actors, expert at how to read to best effect.

Listening to audio means that the experience is being driven by the skills of the narrator in ways that text-to-speech programmes cannot compete. In the UK anything read by Stephen Fry attracts an audience, showing the considerable power of brand names to drive sales. Tom Hanks has narrated his own story collection, *Uncommon Type*, as well as *The Dutch House* by Ann Patchett. George Saunders' *Lincoln in the Bardo* has a cast of many including Lena Dunham, Miranda July, Julianne Moore, Susan Sarandon, David Sedaris, and Ben Stiller. In the USA Penguin Random House increased its audio title output from 650 in 2014 to 1,400 in 2018, and built additional studio capacity for audio.

The opportunity for growth remains significant in English-language markets already well served by choice and quality. Untapped potential is seen in other languages, for example, Spanish. Jorge Reyes of Deyan Audio comments on the challenges:

> You can't compare the two [audio] markets; the English market is so mature, and has dedicated listeners who are addicted to audio and just go from one title to the next. You have to create Spanish listeners, and you create those listeners by creating good content . . . For a lot of people who will buy your audiobook, it will be the first audiobook that they listen to in Spanish. If it's a bad experience, they're gone. (Maughan, 2017, 10)

The arrival of podcasts has been another development, and the more successful ones attract large audiences. 'You cannot talk about trends in audio without mentioning podcasts, and I would say that the latest podcast trend is scripted podcasts; dramatized storytelling in the short episodic podcast format seems to be growing, especially in the US' (Gustafsson, 2021, 7). There is now a wide range of podcast content, often in effect self published. They are available on demand and attract celebrity hosts. The business model is usually that of free to download and they have appealed to younger audiences such as millennials and Gen Z. In the USA in 2020 more than 100 million people over the age of 12 listened regularly to a podcast: 39 per cent of men and 36 per cent of women were regular podcast listeners (Edison Research, 2020).

The podcaster Aaron Mahnke says of the audience for audio: 'Podcast listeners and audiobook listeners share a few common traits. They are busy people who value good story on the go. They understand how intimate audio storytelling can be. And they are modern "readers" who understand the power of technology to inform, to educate, and to entertain' (Klose and Puckett, 2017, 32). The shared audience is confirmed by data in the UK that show that many audiobook listeners also listen to podcasts: this trend is growing with 38 per cent doing so weekly in 2020 compared to 27 per cent in 2017 (Nielsen, 2020, 56).

Whilst there is a definite crossover market between podcasts and audiobooks, book publishers have come relatively late to the party. Nick Jones concludes: 'Since the distinction between podcast and audiobook is ever diminishing in the audience's mind, this represents a very substantial opportunity for audiobook publishers' (2020, 268). As of January 2021, there were 1.75 million podcasts and more than 43 million episodes. The top five countries with the highest penetration of listeners were South Korea, Spain, Sweden, Australia, and the USA (Podcast Insights, 2021). The Amazon-owned Audible has come to dominate the audiobook market in countries such as the USA and the UK: Enders Analysis describes the company as 'a "frenemy" to publishers that has breathed new life into the format but also threatens publishers more in audio than Amazon does in print or e-books' (Edgecliffe-Johnson, 2019).

In the 2020s, the investment in audio started to create new types of experience beyond the single narrator, with experimentation around a cast of actors and dynamic sound effects (Clark and Phillips, 2019). The definition of an audiobook based on a printed book further dissolved with audio-first projects – for example, with writers' rooms creating serialized stories – and the book of the podcast just as there is the book of the film. The fiction podcast has attracted interest from large players such as Netflix and Marvel:

> Many fiction podcasts come with beautiful cinematic musical scores. They also use story devices that make the audio content seem more realistic, anything from secretly recorded conversations to pirate radio broadcasts.

Holy Sh!t uses voice memos exchanged between friends at two different universities to map their story. Fiction podcasts have a fly-on-the-wall feeling that makes them more intimate than other forms of entertainment. (Damon, 2021)

For so long the audiobook was seen as the poor relation of the printed book and yet today it is forging ahead on its own terms, finding new audiences and offering different creative possibilities. As Iben Have and Birgitte Stougaard Pedersen stress, 'we should not discuss the audiobook merely as a re-mediation of the printed book but as an entirely different medium, one that should be conceptualised in relation to mobile media listening practices' (2013, 127).

New Audiences

In the USA, research showed that between 2016 and 2019, the share of adults who had listened to an audiobook grew from 14 per cent to 20 per cent (Pew Research, 2019). As a consequence of technological changes, audio media can be consumed on demand and there is evidence that new generations of listeners are switching from mass-media radio to more personalized podcasts and audiobooks: 'audiobook and podcast listeners skew toward being younger, more educated, and employed – all attributes that make them an attractive customer base' (Deloitte, 2019, 112).

The view of publishers is that ease of listening 'has attracted new customers across a range of demographics, including those who did not previously buy books' (IBIS World, 2021). Richard Lennon from Penguin Random House talks of the audience for audiobooks: 'people who are coming to books and authors often for the first time, or coming back to reading for the first time since they were much younger, and they are coming to audio because of convenience' (Lennon, 2020).

If audio is an entry point for new consumers, that is a way of broadening the customer base of publishers to people who do not necessarily think of themselves as book readers. Richard Lennon sees the audience for audio maturing with a neutral gender balance and some more traditional readers exploring audio. He believes 'it is significant for the publishing industry that audio does seem to skew younger and male because it is an audience that publishing in general is not particularly great at reaching so audio seems to be the primary means of interacting with books for a lot of people who fall into that bracket' (Lennon, 2020).

The challenge for the audio market in the future is to compete effectively with the host of content readily available to consumers. John Thompson writes that audiobooks need to establish a durable presence in the audio-visual mix of digital culture, and even in the audio-only segment, 'audio-books are but one of many options available to consumers: they can listen to music, either from their personal music library on their smartphone or from a streaming service like Spotify, they can listen to any number of radio stations which are now streaming online and they have a huge and growing choice of podcast and podcast services which are advertising-supported and freely available to listeners' (Thompson, 2021, 392).

How does all this relate to the definition of a book that takes reading as one of its main elements? Can it be said that audiobook users are reading audiobooks or is this a self-contradiction? In terms of comprehension and retention, might we expect differences between book reading and book listening? Elaborating in more detail the differences between the two is the starting point for a debate regarding the social status of books.

How Does Listening Differ from Reading?

If we apply a reading-based definition of the book, then an audiobook does not qualify as a book. The narrator is reading the text but this is not the case with the person listening. In today's era of digital files, the audiobook is usually unabridged, ensuring users can listen to the whole text and not a condensed adaptation – but still they are not reading. Listening does not require literacy, neither does it help the listener to become a more fluid reader. It seems unlikely that listening instils the same cognitive patience and focus gained from long-form reading: listeners may be doing the ironing or driving along the motorway, whilst it is difficult (or illegal unless in a driverless vehicle) to try reading a book at the same time.

The insight that the mind may wander more when listening to a story when compared to reading comes from a study comparing silent reading,

reading aloud, and listening. The findings were that 'a more physically engaged reading experience means readers are likely to spend less time mind wandering. In two samples participants reported greater mind wandering when they were simply listening to another individual read, compared to when they engaged in more active forms of information consumption, namely reading silently and aloud' (Sousa et al., 2013, 5). Another study revealed that listening seems to be a more passive way of engaging with narrative than reading, as it involves only one of the senses (Marchetti and Valente, 2018).

The level of comprehension is especially important in settings involving learning in formal education (Baron, 2021). Research in the 1970s tested college students on their comprehension of stories from Boccaccio's *Decameron* – students either read or listened to a story and then had to write up a short summary. There was little difference observed in the quality of the summaries, suggesting reasonable comprehension through either medium. The authors of the study concluded: 'summarizing a story appears to be a fairly complex task and only rather trivial reading-listening differences were observed here . . . One obvious difference between reading and listening which would be highlighted by more difficult texts is the fact that reading rate is usually subject controlled whereas listening rate is not' (Kintsch and Kozminsky, 1977, 498).

Another study amongst university students found that although learners preferred the option of listening as a learning tool, their tested performance was lower than when engaging with the written text (Daniel and Woody, 2010). Cognitive differences may be less pronounced when listening to, for example, fiction or self-help non-fiction (Baron, 2021). Lower performance when listening to educational content might be explained by the results of an investigation into sentence comprehension which concluded that in skilled readers, auditory sentence processing 'inherently imposes greater demands on working memory than does visual sentence process' because 'written language generally allows readers to control the rate of processing, and minimizes demands on working memory by allowing readers to re-read parts of the sentence that were problematic' (Michael et al., 2001, 240).

These findings sit alongside studies suggesting that different parts of the brain are involved with reading and listening. Although both stimulate areas in the left side of the brain associated with language comprehension, other parts of the brain are stimulated by reading (an area associated with the processing of written text) and by listening (an area associated with auditory comprehension) (Michael et al., 2001; Buchweitz et al., 2009). But whilst they can be seen as different activities, this is in no way to pass any value judgement as to their worth: it perhaps means that for different textual content, different types of media are appropriate. For example, if one wants to engage with philosophical texts such as Hegel's *Phenomenology of Spirit* (1807), which requires focus and cognitive patience, reading it in print is likely to be more effective than listening to the audiobook; by comparison, when engaging with a light novel, reading or listening may be equally comfortable.

Sarah Kozloff noted in the 1990s that 'To many, listening to audio books is a debased or lazy way to read, with connotations of illiteracy (only pre-literate children listen to stories); passivity (real reading entails self-construction of the narrative voice); abandonment of control (real reading involves pausing, skimming and savoring); and lack of commitment (real readers sacrifice other activities for their books)' (Kozloff, 1995, 83). But were such views simply reflecting a snobbery on the part of book readers who may have been happy to listen to speech radio and broadcast plays? Could part of the contemporary boom in audio be because this is *not* reading books – it is a different activity away from what is seen as a more elitist and cognitively more demanding pursuit? There is an undoubted attraction towards audio from new audiences. But why might book reading be seen as a somewhat high-brow pursuit? How does this relate to the special status of books in contemporary society?

5 The Social and Cultural Status of the Book

The evidence that books have a special status in contemporary society is not hard to find. There are measures in many countries to support the diversity of book production and to facilitate access to books: the public library system is the most visible and globally widespread mechanism for supporting reading habits, followed by zero or reduced rates of VAT (e.g. in the UK), fixed prices for books to prevent discounting and maintain a wide network of bookstores (e.g. in France and Germany), and support for print runs (e.g. in Norway). In the European Union the framework programme Creative Europe promotes literary translation and many countries have special grant programmes for book authors, translators, book editors, and literary agents.

Such measures date back to the early twentieth century, even to the nineteenth century in some countries (Feather, 1988), and were the norm in most countries at the beginning of the twenty-first century (Ronning and Slaatta, 2019 and 2020). The main reason for the introduction of such policies is the belief that books are 'a strategic commodity that activates the knowledge economy' because they bring 'long-term social, cultural and economic benefits' to societies (IPA-FEP, 2019).

However, not all books are bearers of knowledge: Hitler and Stalin, to name two of the most notorious examples, were authors of widely popular books that spread hatred, prejudice, and bias. Many books are poorly written and some struggle to satisfy any need for entertainment and have little to do with imparting knowledge. Nevertheless, regulatory interventions are applied to all books regardless of their content and quality. The main – and convincing – argument for such an all-encompassing book policy is that having government agencies assess the quality of books for tax exemption purposes would be time-consuming, expensive, and complicated – and would reek of censorship.

Book policies are therefore executed in such a way that some books are able to piggyback on the shoulders of others. Whilst other creative industries are important for human well-being and creativity too, no direct all-encompassing policies are applied in the same way to film, television, architecture, art, craft, design, software, or games. Funding policies are instead targeted at specific projects or categories of products and services, for example tax breaks for film production. The question what is a book could therefore be reformulated: who 'programmed' books in such a way (and when did this happen) that they have a special status in the contemporary media landscape and where do these, largely invisible, 'factory presets' of the book come from? In Western civilization, these default settings come from the Order of the Book, as proposed by Adriaan van der Weel.

Order of the Book

The Order of the Book is defined by the codes of print that differ significantly from the codes of textual transmission as they existed in societies prior to print, much as the invention of writing produced a change in communication patterns in oral cultures (Goody and Watt, 1968; Ong, 1982; Havelock, 1986). The consequences of the change from oral to written communication manifested themselves in many ways. First of all, writing allowed for the dissemination of information in a tangible form beyond time and place, which was not the case with oral communication: 'knowledge became independent from the person who held that knowledge' (van der Weel, 2011, 78) and could be shared amongst those who could read and write without the need for contact between the sender and receiver of the information. The written record allowed for the assessment of one person's observations by another who might be distant in time and space from the first, leading to the possibility of greater objectivity on one hand and greater precision of formulation on the other: 'The realisation that a reader may dissect the verbal tissue of thoughts after gaining access to them in a material form could not but tend to a greater exactness of expression in the writing process' (78). Following Julian Jaynes' argumentation in *The Origin of Consciousness in the Breakdown of the Bicameral Mind*, van der Weel suggests that the invention of writing had the side effect of enabling individuals to 'look at themselves from the outside, so that they become capable of seeing themselves as distinct persons with a particular past, and directing themselves towards a particular imagined future on the basis of their own judgements and decisions' (76).

Writing, then, fostered the development of consciousness: of course language provides the primary tool that makes this possible, but the invention of writing augmented this process. As Jaynes points out, the ancient Greek aphorism to 'know thyself' inscribed on the forecourt of the temple of Apollo at Delphi 'would have been something inconceivable to the Homeric heroes' who lived in times of purely oral communication (Jaynes, 2000, 287). The invention of printing was both a continuation and an evolution of these processes. Combined with the socio-economic circumstances that began to favour entrepreneurship and the spread of literacy in late medieval and early modern Europe, printing transformed the transmission of text in four directions. These form the backbone of our understanding of what a book is and what it does in Western societies.

First, thanks to printing, textual production exploded after 1450. Although it is impossible to calculate the exact increase in the number of copies and titles in circulation after the invention of printing compared to the manuscript era (Krummel, 2013), the circumstantial evidence is solid. The aim of the Library of Alexandria was to collect all known texts of antiquity and this remained the ideal model of a library until the end of the Middle Ages. Two millennia later and less than a century after the invention of printing, Conrad Gessner attempted to compile a bibliography (rather than texts in their materiality) of all scientific works written in Latin, Greek, or Hebrew, the languages of science at the time. He gave up after publishing three volumes as the number of printed books was simply increasing too rapidly for basic bibliographic data on them to be collected with the tools available in the early modern period (see van der Weel, 2011, 74–5). This proliferation continued and accelerated well into our own time: between 1911 and 2009, the number of published titles grew from 10 million to 168 million. With the growth of print-on-demand services and the introduction of Amazon's Kindle, the production of new titles received a significant boost (Kovač and Wischenbart, 2019). Despite the presence of a range of data-gathering methods, due to the explosive growth of newly published titles and lack of adequate statistical tools, the compilation of book statistics in many countries remains uneven (Kovač et al., 2017).

Secondly, the capacity of books to store text has increased throughout the era of printing whilst their prices have decreased. Printed editions of the Bible from the fifteenth and sixteenth centuries, for example, weigh at least five times more than a copy of the Bible found in some hotel rooms today.

The price of Gutenberg's Bible in the fifteenth century was equivalent to the price of a stone villa in Mainz (Kapr, 1996), whilst the prices of many printed books today do not exceed the price of a meal at a fast-food restaurant. As a result, the sheer volume of information started to increase rapidly from the first centuries of printing: information overload was something to complain about already by the eighteenth century (Blair, 2011). It is worth noting that such long-lasting developments in print culture correspond with – much faster – trends in the digital landscape as described by Moore's and Kryder's Laws, that the prices of digital technologies are falling whilst their processing power and storage capacity are increasing (Kovač, 2008).

Thirdly, it was in the nature of printing that the content in the copies of the same text in the same edition was identical. As noted by many book historians, in the early centuries of printing, technical difficulties with the presses led to discrepancies between copies of the same edition (Johns, 1998; Raven, 2019). However, these differences were minor and did not challenge the appearance of standardization. Van der Weel argues that this standardization of content was an intended consequence of printing and was welcomed by the church because of efforts to standardize the liturgy. The identicalness of individual pages, however, was an unintended and to some extent undesirable effect of printing, since in the eyes of contemporaries it 'turned books into industrial, "off the rack" products compared with the bespoke nature of the manuscript book' (van der Weel, 2011, 85). In the words of Walter Benjamin, the printed book was becoming a non-auratic object in comparison to its auratic manuscript predecessor.

Despite not necessarily being welcome, the identicalness of the page had long-lasting and profound consequences: pagination, indexes, and content pages were established, which offered 'convenient ways into the texts and made a crucial contribution to the *machine à lire* that the book has since become' (van der Weel, 2011, 85). Through the stability of the page, the information architecture of the book as described in Chapter 3 was made possible. In addition, the book information architecture required consistency and standardization in the organization of textual content – prerequisites for analytical and scientific thinking. The book as a content machine was thus ideally suited to the storage and dissemination of scholarly knowledge as it started to evolve in modern-age Europe. By this, the book become a central medium of culture and science for centuries. As we shall see in the Conclusion, this central position started to dissolve in the late twentieth and early twenty-first centuries.

Fourthly, the printed book has proven resilient because a business model emerged in the early days of printing that still works for the supply chain today. As we shall see in Chapter 7, this business model became an important part of the media identity of the book. The long-lasting security of the business model has made physical bookshops a part of the urban landscape and enabled them to survive to the present, when many other types of retail, such as music stores, have left the high street. Examples of long-established bookstores include Livraria Bertrand in Lisbon (1732), the Galignani bookstore in Paris (1801), and the bookstore at 23, Rynek Główny in Krakow that has – run by a set of different owners – operated in the same house since 1610.

From the eighteenth century onwards this enduring business model gave birth to copyright laws. By granting the owner the exclusive right to make copies of a creative work, and by inventing concepts such as moral rights and the exhaustion of rights, a set of rules allowed the business of publishing to operate in a sustainable way transparent to all parties. These rules have since been applied to other media industries and still govern the way many media products are produced, sold, and distributed. In addition to copyright rules, basic publishing terms in wide use today – such as publisher, author, publication, and (web) page – can also be seen as evidence of the bookish origins of today's media culture.

As a consequence of these four major changes in the transmission of texts there emerged the protocols for how textual knowledge is formatted, transmitted, and exchanged. The most visible manifestations of these protocols, based on identicalness of the page and the information architecture of the book, are copyright rules, standardization of knowledge, and book policy measures. As already mentioned, these protocols and the materiality of print in which they were embedded were one of the infrastructural preconditions for the development and spread of knowledge as it occurred in the modern era. As Elizabeth Eisenstein proposed in her seminal work *The Printing Press As an Agent of Change* (1980), it became much easier for early modern scholars with access to libraries of printed books to discuss the same textual content, compare interpretations, and find errors in data and reasoning than it was for their manuscript-era predecessors, who had to travel from one library to another to access books and to memorize or write down their contents before departure. In such circumstances, analytical reading was almost a mission impossible. Print made possible different interpretations of works that were considered in the manuscript era absolute truths; also, by printing different manuscript versions of authoritative works, it became clear that authors who were considered ultimate authorities in their field sometimes contradicted themselves.

As a result, the identicalness of the page and the proliferation of textual production led to instability in interpretations of readings with profound cultural and social consequences. Differing readings sometimes fomented religious wars, as was the case in seventeenth-century Europe during the Thirty Years' War. Over time the clash of different interpretations came to be seen as something that brought new knowledge to light – in turn disseminated through print and feeding new growth in knowledge. Of course, analytical and scientific thought appeared in other civilizations and cultures – and in Europe before the printing press. But the amalgam of socio-economic circumstances in early modern Europe in combination with printing technologies made the dissemination of analytical thought, combined with the standardization and consistency of information, much easier and more widespread than through any other information tool in any other era or in any other civilization. Without the printing press, the Age of Enlightenment would most likely have been a minor and sporadic local occurrence in European history.

Changes in the media landscape walked hand in hand with broader social transformations in Western civilization. With the growth of the market economy in the eighteenth and nineteenth centuries, the bureaucratic organization of states and societies emerged, requiring standardized and consistent information (Weber, 1905). As a result, mass education based on book-formatted content became considered one of the pillars of social and economic development. Further, in the second half of the twentieth century, in many societies the role of the knowledge economy became emphasized on the assumption that the growth of economies depended on innovation in products and services (Drucker, 1999). A key requirement for citizens was to be educated sufficiently to navigate social rules and have sufficient knowledge and expertise to contribute to the economy. Mass certification and mass education came to be seen as vital elements of the modern economy (Graeber, 2016). In order to access professional jobs, people have to acquire certifiable knowledge – and at least until the early days of the digital era, this knowledge was presented through the codes and protocols of the Order of the Book. In contemporary educational parlance, we call this book-based knowledge literacy. Of course literacy goes beyond the ability to read books to the reading of a host of documents and objects: signs, manuals, guides, contracts, advertisements, printed tickets, pamphlets, schedules, programmes, tax reports, insurance documents, employment contracts, reports. These products of writing and printing have multiplied over the past few centuries, making life hard without the ability to navigate them. The typewriter, telex, fax, offset printing, and digital technology all helped to solidify the textual underpinnings of society. We now do more functional reading than ever before in human history (see van der Weel, 2011, 98–100), and understanding regulations and instructions, submitting reports and applications, and writing and reading emails are all vital for forging a path in today's world.

Literacy and the Order of the Book are not just the province of democratic societies. Associated policies around bureaucracy and education are also required to stabilize and perpetuate the power of authoritarian regimes. Perhaps this helps us understand why dictators of the twentieth century – Stalin, Mao, and Hitler – felt the urge to write books, which in turn played an important role in their rise to power, even though they largely used radio and film to communicate with the masses (Sebag Montefiore, 2003; Chang and Halliday, 2007; Kershaw 2010). The banishment of 'degenerate' authors from the public sphere and the burning of books in authoritarian regimes show how their proponents were not only aware of the power of books to spread critical and analytical thought that might undermine the regime's authority. They were also aware that in the Order of the Book, the prestige of authorship adds weight to the leader's power and charisma that in authoritarian societies often becomes a substitute for the lack of democratic institutions. More recently Barack Obama, Boris Johnson, and Donald Trump are book authors (although the last may well not have read his own books; see M. Trump, 2020), suggesting that even today in democratic societies, the Order of the Book radiates prestige that goes hand in hand with political power.

Machines That Made Us

All this leads to the conclusion that throughout the modern age, the book became an invisible machine that formatted the mental fabric of societies dependent on the spread of certifiable knowledge, information, and innovation. In the words of Stephen Fry (2008), the book is a machine that made us – and precisely because of its formative role in how we think and feel, the book and its formatting properties became invisible to most of us. That we can now see the contours of the rationale that made possible the blind spot around which the Order of the Book is structured may therefore be an indicator of its approaching end. In other words, in the digital age we can recognize the lack of clarity around notions such as bookishness and aura of the book because we are looking at the Order of the Book from a changed media and social perspective. A plurality of printers, publishers, and booksellers is being replaced by a coterie of tech companies benefitting from the network effects of an always-on society and economy, the belief that copyright is an obstacle rather than an enabling protocol in information societies, and the irrelevance of the formatting powers of print for the Web: these are striking signs that the codes and protocols of the Order of the Book are losing their framing grip in contemporary society.

In the Order of the Book, the main mode of acquiring knowledge is reading. This brings us back to the questions we asked when analysing the differences between print and audiobooks. What is reading and how does its 'elitist' status relate to the Order of the Book? How has reading and its meaning changed in a digital landscape?

6 Does Reading Still Matter?

A word of caution is necessary at the outset: both reading history and reading are slippery research areas. For one thing, reading is an activity that leaves few material traces and is therefore difficult to research. For another, reading has rarely been considered an activity worth describing and observing by those who practised it. As a result, there is mostly only circumstantial evidence of how people in history have read, how they interacted with different forms of text, and what kind of thoughts and emotions were triggered by reading. Nonetheless, with the help of such evidence and thanks to the empirical research on reading that started to take place in the second half of the twentieth century, a number of reading historians, psychologists, and neuroscientists have provided a compelling narrative of how reading evolved and changed (see Cavalho and Chartier, 1999; Fischer, 2003; Lyons, 2010; Towheed et al., 2011; Furedi, 2015; Willingham, 2017; Wolf, 2018).

Empirical research on reading comprehension, however, usually in relation to reading substrates, inherently has a number of limitations. For example, if two people with different educational backgrounds and reading habits are reading the Booker winner by Damon Galgut, it is very likely that the person with a university degree in literature will read the book faster and with a higher level of comprehension than a person with a professional degree whose reading is limited to web surfing and romance or thrillers. But what if the literature graduate is reading the novel from a smartphone and the one with the professional degree is reading a printed book? And what if the reader with the literature degree reads in the evening after a long working day, and the person with the professional degree uses their pandemic lockdown time to resurrect reading as a pastime? Obviously, such differences in reading time, mode, and substrate influence the level of reading comprehension and make reading research a complex enterprise.

Because of such factors, experiments in reading comprehension often involve a few dozen volunteer readers with similar backgrounds who read the same texts under the same circumstances and at the same time of day. As a result, the longest texts read in the research are usually no longer than one chapter of a book and the experiments are often conducted with undergraduates, the most accessible population for researchers. These limitations require caution when interpreting research studies and highlight the importance of meta-studies that summarize the results of a large number of similar experiments on reading.

Evolution of Reading

With these methodological issues in mind, let us begin by noting that reading has a long and erratic history. In the early days of writing, most non-functional reading was done aloud and in public. Even centuries later, in the Middle Ages, the Bible and other religious texts were read aloud in monasteries during meals. In rural areas in Europe, such readings survived until the nineteenth century, when people gathered in their homes in the evening and usually listened to the only villager who could read fluently. Since few texts were available in ancient times and the Middle Ages, the same works were read over and over again. This type of reading is called intensive controlled reading because listeners cannot choose what they read nor can they individually adjust their listening speed or pause when they want to think about something (Carmody, 2010).

These reading patterns persisted as mainstream well into the first centuries of printing and only began to disappear at the time of the Industrial Revolution with the growth of urbanization and the invention of the steam-powered printing press, which made it possible to print books quickly, in larger quantities, and at lower cost. As stressed in Chapter 5, the development of commerce required more people to be able to read and write, leading to the introduction of compulsory primary education and, in our days, to mass certification. This new readership had enough money and leisure time to read occasionally either for education or for entertainment, and new genres of books emerged, intended for mass, usually recreational and individual, reading. People read silently, alone, at their own pace, and often without any external control over their selection of books. Novels, poems, fairy tales, plays, political and philosophical treatises – all these books provided a choice of reading material. Reading became a means of entertainment, an instrument of education or social mobility, essential training for thinking or possibly a breeding ground for subversive ideas: without the printing press and the spread of literacy, there would doubtless have been no French or Russian Revolution.

This type of reading was transformed with the advent of digital media. In order to understand the nature of this change, we need to take a quick look at the cognitive process of reading.

Reading As a Cognitive Process

What is happening in our brains when we read? Simply put, cognitive processes consist of sensory, working, and long-term memory. Each plays a role in processing information – and in reading. Sensory memory allows us to take in different types of information through the senses (eyes, ears, nose, mouth, and skin), which is then processed in working memory, 'a work space where thought happens' (Willingham, 2017, 65). Once processed, the information is stored in long-term memory, from where we can retrieve it as required. So when we read, we process information in working memory and store it in long-term memory.

The first requirement for reading is learning the alphabet. At first glance, this does not seem to be a particularly difficult challenge since Western alphabets have only around thirty letters. But learning the alphabet is not enough; you also have to learn how to associate letters with sounds, and that is no longer a trivial task: 'People have regional accents, and two people ostensibly saying the same thing can produce quite different speech sounds,' Willingham writes. An 'individual speaker also says them differently, depending on the context' (36). The difference between 'pee' and 'bee', for example, is slight when you hear the isolated words, and associating the right sound with the right letter may require more context. When learning to read, we have to learn to hear the sounds in words that sound different in different dialects. It is even more difficult to learn how to hear the words and sentences in speech because 'brief pauses between words don't really exist in the speech stimulus' (35). Without hearing words in speech, we cannot hear sounds in words, and without hearing sounds in words, we cannot associate them with letters, which is a prerequisite for reading. Literate people have this experience when they learn a foreign language. For example, someone who is not proficient in English is unlikely to hear the letter i in the word Mike because the letter i is associated with different sounds in English than in, say, Polish or Slovenian. Similarly, a native speaker of English with no knowledge of Polish, Slovene, or Icelandic would have serious problems associating sounds with letters when confronted with names such as that of the Polish village of Szymankowszczyzna or the Slovenian town of Jesenice, not to mention the longest word in Icelandic: Vaðlaheiðarvegavinnuverkfærageymsluskúrslyklakippuhrin gurinn.

The Transformation of Reading in the Era of Screens

The capacity of working memory is limited and we are not able to do more than a few tasks at a time. When we have a problem with spelling, we overload our working memory so that it no longer has the capacity to process the content of what we read. This limited capacity can be outsmarted by acquiring certain mental skills so that its work becomes automatic. This frees up space in the working memory and makes it available for cognitive work: our reading skills therefore must become automatic if we want to process the meaning of what is being read in working memory. We can assume that during the growth of print production and mass literacy in the modern age a growing percentage of the population became automatic readers through constant reading, which enabled them to process reading content easily. As we have shown in the discussion of audio, by listening to audio content, we do not enhance such decoding and comprehension skills. Listening is a different cognitive process and this puts a question mark against the belief that audiobooks should be parts of literacy programmes and that removing 'the restraints of a student's word recognition and decoding skills provides a very positive approach to focusing on the meaning behind an author's words' (Wolfson, 2008). In other words, simply through listening we do not become automatic readers since an audiobook can be listened to by an illiterate person: listening is thus unlikely to improve their reading skills.

A greater facility with reading enables a variety of modes of reading, and we will focus on deep reading, immersive reading and skimming (see Wolf and Brazillai, 2009; Baron, 2015; Kovač and van der Weel, 2018; Wolf, 2018). Whilst we read, we not only automatically decode words, we also process their meaning and contexts and compare them to what is stored in our long-term memory. As educated adults, we can simulate this experience by learning a foreign language or reading a sophisticated text, say from a branch of science with which we are not familiar. In this case we are not struggling with the recognition of sounds and letters in spoken words – as we did when trying to read the Polish word Szymankowszczyzna – but with the meaning of words. The fewer foreign words or scientific terms with their meanings we have stored in long-term memory, the more trouble we have automatically guessing their meaning when we encounter them in a text, and the less room there is in working memory to process the meaning of sentences we read or hear. Conversely, the more words we understand, the more space our working memory has free to process what we read. Some studies have shown that not understanding 2 per cent of the words in the text is enough to give problems understanding the text as a whole (Willingham, 2017, 90). This is true not only when we read in a foreign language we do not know well, or when a book historian tries to understand quantum mechanics. It is also the case if someone who understands a small number of words and has limited reading ability reads a simple text in their native language, such as a TV set manual. Widening the vocabulary of words one understands is therefore one of the prerequisites for thinking.

Yet understanding the meanings of many words does not help much if we do not have stored in our long-term memory grammatical rules and the factual and procedural knowledge that connects the meanings of the words we read into meaningful sentences. This knowledge enables us to understand that there is a web of connections between concepts whereby the same word can change its meanings in different textual, social, and historical contexts. (For example, the verb scroll can mean to roll or unroll a sheet of paper or to move through a page on a computer screen.) When we become able to navigate amongst the different meanings of the same word, we deepen our vocabulary.

To obtain this kind of knowledge it is necessary to focus long enough to process what one has read: reading of longer texts cannot occur without the mental stamina to pay sustained attention to what we read. The ability to read automatically, a depth and breadth of vocabulary, the facility to use rules of logic, and the ability to focus could be thus seen as basic prerequisites for being able to express complex thoughts; up until now, humanity has found no other way to develop such abilities and such knowledge than by reading. The deep reading of longer and more complex texts is therefore training for thinking and for acquiring new knowledge, even if we are not reading for learning purposes. In the context of the Order of the Book, the book is the most natural medium for this kind of reading, leading to its traditional, central position in education and in knowledge dissemination. As Adam Garfinkle (2021) comments: 'Beyond self-inflicted attention deficits, people who cannot deep read – or who do not use and hence lose the deep-reading skills they learned – typically suffer from an attenuated capability to comprehend and use abstract reasoning. In other words, if you can't, or don't, slow down sufficiently to focus quality attention – what [Maryanne] Wolf calls "cognitive patience" – on a complex problem, you cannot effectively think about it.'

Yet not all immersive reading is necessarily deep reading in a way that deepens and broadens vocabulary or enables abstract and strategic reasoning. When a skilled reader reads genre fiction, for example, they may be immersed in a text without significantly broadening and deepening their vocabulary. The reader simply enjoys the content in the same way that a moviegoer is immersed in a film or a video gamer is immersed in a computer game. Yet it is impossible to make a clear distinction between categories of books that evoke immersive and deep reading because the reading process is a highly subjective activity. For example, if a native English speaker learns Latvian and reads a novel by Dan Brown in that language, this could be considered deep reading because they encounter new words and grammatical rules and transfer familiar worlds into new linguistic contexts. If they read the same book in their native language, such reading would most likely be simply immersive.

A shift in modes of reading occurred with the arrival of the personal computer, tablet, and smartphone, a new set of communication tools. In turn there sprung up a host of new media – and because there are only twenty-four hours in a day, TikTok, Instagram, YouTube, blogs, apps, and so on have taken attention away from newspapers, books, radio, and the established TV stations. Since much of the new media is based on the written word, we are probably reading more than ever before. The result is that reading has become even more extensive than in the days when print media dominated. This has led to a new form of reading known as skimming (Liu, 2005; Wolf, 2018).

Skimming involves readers quickly responding to online content without much thought, or any checking of the source, or wondering about the motives behind its dissemination. In addition, much of social media is addictive (Vaidhyanathan, 2018) as it creates the need for constant information stimuli. These stimuli are all the more effective because they can be personalized, and the algorithms that drive social media often know more about our reactions to different types of information than we do, trapping us in information bubbles – we see predominantly the content that stimulates us most. One of the many lessons of digital transformation is that bias and hate are more stimulative than more positive feelings, making the pair today at home in social media.

Yet hate and bias are not inherent, unavoidable properties of digital media, neither is skimming per se a harmful activity. It should not be forgotten that analogue media was also susceptible to manipulation and falsehoods: as previously mentioned, the history of totalitarian and authoritarian regimes in Europe in the twentieth century indicates that by using the protocols and codes of the Order of the Book, it was possible to trap entire populations in a huge information bubble by using heavily controlled print and audiovisual media that build their appeal on bias and hate. In addition, skimming is a highly useful technique for finding and selecting information at speed – we also use it when examining printed texts. From a cognitive perspective, therefore, in combination with deep reading, skimming could enhance our ability to understand, manipulate, and navigate a sea of information. However, if it displaces those types of reading that deepen and broaden vocabulary, skimming may indeed erode thinking abilities. Such a step would probably mean, at worst, an abrupt end to the Order of the Book, with no one left capable of observing and understanding its decline; or, at best, the emergence of a new cognitive order in which people acquire knowledge and develop thinking abilities in ways and with tools that we cannot fully understand from our current historical, book-determined perspective.

In short, the special role of the book in contemporary societies comes from its central role in the dissemination of knowledge. This knowledge could be either rationalist, skeptical knowledge or knowledge necessary, say, for indoctrination into an ideology. As long as knowledge connects to power, the Order of the Book is an inescapable concept in understanding power relations as they emerged in Western societies: for example, working-class libraries were seen as an important tool in the struggle for social equality in the late nineteenth and early twentieth centuries (Rose, 2010). The increasingly marginalized role of the research monograph by comparison to journal publication (Thompson, 2005) indicates a minor transformation but could also be seen as a symptom of broader cultural change.

Such a broad range of perspectives allows us to link the technical definition of the book to the social and cultural dynamic that led to its formulation. If we look at skimming, immersive, and deep reading from the perspective of the Order of the Book, deep reading holds a central position: without it, books would not be carriers of knowledge, be it rationalist or not. In the context of the Order of the Book, deep reading is seen as an elite mode of reading as it is one of the main ways of acquiring knowledge. Being seen as a book reader thus means being seen as a person who is at the very heart of literacy and knowledge: the need of oligarchs and politicians to appear surrounded by books and even to become authors is in turn connected with the power structures of societies interwoven with the protocols of the Order of the Book. The elitist attitude of book readers towards other types of consumption of textual information is inherent to the Order of the Book. The negative connotations of such elitism can be seen as a sign of the Order's diminishing importance.

To sum up, from the perspective of the Order of the Book, the most bookish object is the printed book, as defined by UNESCO and the USPS since it can be read deeply and immersively or just skimmed, and as long as it stimulates deep reading, it should be considered one of the most important tools for the transfer of knowledge, deserving of special status. Close to the printed book is the e-book, which can also be accessed via all three reading modes. However, a number of meta-studies (Singer and Alexander, 2017; Delgado et al., 2018; Clinton, 2019) conclude that screen technologies are less suited to deep reading, suggesting the e-book is a book object of the second order often used for immersive reading.

As we have seen, there have been few studies on the differences between audiobooks, e-books, and printed books regarding cognition and the understanding of content: given the fast growth in audio, it is likely that this will become an important area of research. On the basis of present knowledge, however, it is safe to assume that audiobooks offer immersion in long-form narratives but appear less likely than print to stimulate deep thinking. Moreover, as stressed in the discussion of audio, we do not read audiobooks, so no automatic reading is needed or practised; indeed, for listening to audiobooks, it is not necessary to be literate. Yet a book in audio format has exactly the same narrative and the vocabulary with exactly the same depth and breadth as the same book in printed format. From the perspective of the Order of the Book, audiobooks therefore align as a third-order object – and if they lack the information architecture of the book, they leave the book family entirely. Silent books do allow immersion in a story, but there is no reading, no textual narrative, and no new vocabulary; accordingly, they should be considered an object of the fourth order. Whilst colouring books are a book-like artefact, there is no story, no reading, and no vocabulary: they evoke other, non-textual kinds of immersion. We therefore consider them as a book object of the fifth order. The following diagram (see Figure 2) shows the hierarchy of book objects as they exist in the Order of the Book.

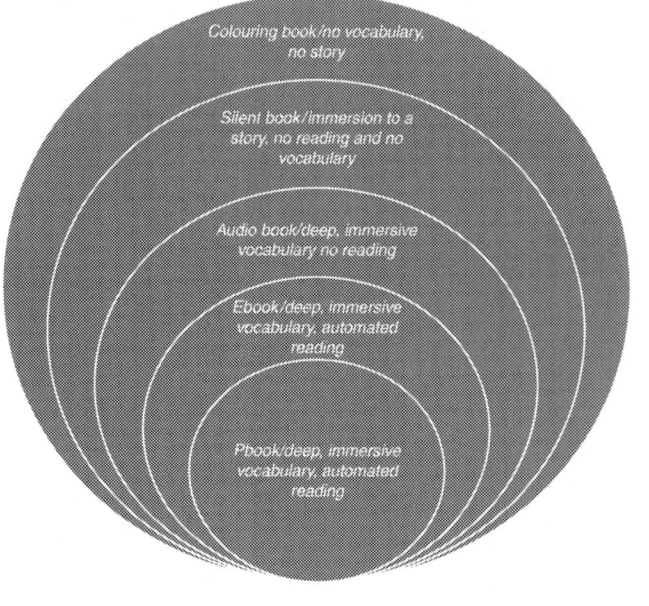

Figure 2 The Order of the Book

All these forms of the book have one more thing in common: a business model whose legal, cultural, and economic framework is determined by properties of the printed book and by the protocols of the Order of the Book.

7 The Book As Business Model

The Internet is an enormously powerful publishing platform and much content previously published in book form has been replaced by online information, often user generated. There are a number of routes for self-expression and self-publishing, from social media to newsletters and pod-casts. How then do we distinguish between content in book form and similar content on the Web? The definition from the *Oxford English Dictionary* (see Chapter 1) suggested that a written composition long enough to fill a printed volume constitutes a book. But where does that leave fiction posted online or a series of blog posts on a certain topic? We are reluctant to call such texts a book. Surely there is a way of separating out different publishing approaches and formats.

Home reference, maps, and travel are examples of categories in con-sumer publishing where much content has gone online. A significant pro-portion of research monographs, textbooks, and schoolbooks may migrate to digital, with books broken up into chapters that look like journal papers or replaced by bite-sized content. Such change is the result of a variety of forces including the ease of access of digital resources, declining budgets for print, the arrival of open access in academic books, piracy, rental schemes for textbooks, and second-hand sales. As stressed in Chapter 1, this process matches the agenda of the container theorists who view the book as a parcel of content ripe for unbundling.

If the same content can be parcelled up in different ways, whether on a website or in a book, is then the difference around the business model? The web business model mostly benefits the tech companies. Google is keen for content to be free and discoverable – they make their money from advertising and click-throughs, not from selling the content – again not the business model of the book. Stories on a platform such as Wattpad are not books – they have a different business model with free access and income from advertising or the sponsorship of stories. They do offer publishers the advantage of market testing of stories and authors, however, just as was the case with serialized fiction in the nineteenth century: 'Great profits could be gained from successful serials as they would increase the number of readers. Another undeniable advantage was that the practice allowed publishers to test novels before publishing them in book form' (Marie-Françoise Cachen in Raven, 2020, 293).

Viewing the book as a business model separates it from a serial publication like a journal or magazine. Chapters and journal articles presented online become indistinguishable to the reader when part of a vast database. But the business model for journals is different to that of the copy sale model of the book (Clark and Phillips, 2019), with high fixed costs for digital platforms and traditionally relying on subscriptions paid in advance and little or no payment to authors. The open-access model of journals often relies on monies from library and research budgets or project funding. An upmarket magazine resembles a book in colour – bound and with quality text and ravishing illustrations – yet the business model is very different, relying on advertising to supplement the income from the subscription or cover price.

The Book As Business Model

What is the business model of the book? It involves payment by a customer for a product in print or digital form. It involves an act of publication, an investment in the author and the product, protected by copyright law to the benefit of the author and publisher. The imprint of the publisher gives validation to the author's work, a mark of quality and commercial potential. Curation of a publishing list (Bhaskar, 2016) offers readers access to quality content, an approach in contrast to the content abundance model of the Internet. 'The traditional book publishing model is built on a process of selection whereby publishers screen many authors and manuscripts and select those that seem most likely to achieve minimum sales targets ... Publishers are most interested in books they can print in quantity for sale to large audiences' (Osterwalder and Pigneur, 2010, 70). Publishers also serve niche audiences, whether through small print runs at higher prices (e.g. academic books) or single copies printed to order (e.g. backlist titles).

Perhaps rather surprisingly, the business model of the printed book has remained relatively stable and has proved reliable for the past three hundred years. It does not rely on advertising and in the supply chain discounts are given to specialized intermediaries (such as wholesalers and bookstores) to encourage the distribution, marketing, and stockholding of books. Darnton's communication circuit summarized the players en route from author to reader (and back to the author) as they existed in the eighteenth century, and to a great extent they remain the same today in (print) trade publishing (Darnton, 1982). The printed book offers the template for the model, relying on the economics of the printing press (economies of scale) and giving the parameters for what is creatively possible and financially viable. The financial risk of publication is held by the publisher and the author shares in this risk by agreeing to take a royalty share according to sales. The financial risk of one book is balanced out by the risks taken across a publishing list, or across a diversified set of lists across subject areas or categories of publishing. In trade publishing one huge success may mitigate the losses incurred from a number of other titles. As Roberto Calasso suggested, 'we are forced to consider the idea that the capacity to make people read (or at least *buy*) certain books is a key factor in the quality of a publishing house. The market – or the relationship with that unknown, obscure being known as *the public* – is the first ordeal of the publisher, in the medieval sense of the word: a test of fire that can send a considerable amount of money up in smoke' (2015, 11).

As we have seen in the first chapter, the book as a CD-ROM or an app did not lack creativity or investment – the book business model failed since the revenues against consumer expectations around price failed to cover the costs of production, this in a format with few of the boundaries of the printed book (Phillips, 2014). Similarly the digital book as adventure game disappeared in the direction of gaming – again a different business model with the expectation of reaching many players. The multitude of books published reflects the workings of the business model even with low print runs. As Gabriel Zaid remarked, 'the economic threshold, or the minimum investment required to gain access to the market, is very low, which encourages the proliferation of titles and publishing houses, the flourishing of various and disparate initiatives, and an abundance of cultural richness. If the threshold of viability were as high as it is for the mass media, there would be less diversity, as is true of mass media' (Zaid, 2004, 26–7). The arrival of the e-book has accelerated the proliferation of books with many self-published titles available, and digital formats and digital printing mean that books no longer need go out of print. The golfer Padraig Harrington sees the flip side of the high output from publishers:

> It's a tough business, a rat race. It's nearly like estate agents. For a publisher to sell an extra 5% of books takes a lot of effort so they're almost as well doing another book with somebody else. Roll out the next book, don't push the current one. I wanted to get information out there and the way the world is now, you just go and do it yourself on social media.' (Murray, 2020)

There are undoubtedly benefits from the neat boundaries of the business model of the book. Craig Mod summarizes the purchasing transaction as it exists in the contemporary book business: 'We buy a book, we know what we're getting. There is no other "business model" at play. No other information being (necessarily, relatively) sold. This clarity of contract is especially lucid in physical form. The book has edges. The transaction has edges. The transaction completes. Given time, we complete the book. It has an ending. Contracts are clear. Usually, there's no tracking' (Mod, 2019). The printed edition has an ownership model allowing us to pass books on to family and friends or the charity shop. The business model relies on selling copies for gifting to others for birthdays and holiday seasons – mostly in print. But we also gift to ourselves when we buy a nicely produced book or the latest hardback novel from our favourite author. The business model is not a model of usage since some copies are sold but never read at all – at home or from public libraries. Of print books on our shelves at home, it is estimated that only half have been read (Clark and Phillips, 2019). As seen earlier, there is similar behaviour amongst readers of e-books.

The lending of books is also part of the business model of books. In many countries libraries support reading habits through their purchasing of print books; however, we do not have enough data to conclude that such policies support book sales. In consumer publishing some evidence runs in the opposite direction (Kovač, 2008), and a 2019 study in Germany found that after joining an e-book library system, around half of the patrons purchased significantly fewer books or no books at all (GfK, 2019). Hardback editions in particular are bought by public and academic libraries and in many countries a system of public lending right offers some return to authors for library borrowings. There is further state support through the sourcing of educational textbooks for schoolchildren and purchasing may be centralized by region or country, which undoubtedly helps family budgets, but it remains open whether such measures are indeed supporting the business model of publishers.

The vanilla e-book is free from the length and physical constraints of the physical book but retains the central business model. Rather than sell one, larger e-book, authors and publishers see the advantages of discrete titles that can be sold separately. A supply of new titles also encourages the sale of the more established titles in the publisher's backlist (Berglund and Steiner, 2021). The same principle works for self-published works, as remarked on by Mike Shatzkin: 'All of the best self-published writers – or the most successful ones – say that one of the key things is to be prolific. Keep feeding the beast, because what happens is you get fans, and they will keep buying the stuff you make available. But if you stop, they will forget about you' (Phillips, 2014, 5).

The ecosystem of the e-book offers a potentially different business model of low pricing without the offer to the consumer of ownership – in this access model, e-books are read under a licence. Lower pricing reduces the risk for readers and works well in categories such as genre fiction where readers have high levels of consumption. It also works for mainstream publishers when they introduce new authors to the market, and for self-published authors for whom there is no prospect of distributing their works in print format through high street shops. Streaming options such as the service Kindle Unlimited, giving access to a large number of titles in return for a monthly subscription (the model has echoes of the circulating libraries of the eighteenth and nineteenth centuries), move the business model away from the copy sale model to one where revenues to author and publisher depending on usage. The streaming model is still met with caution by publishers and as John Thompson highlights: 'In any subscription model ... it is the heavy users who have the most to gain ... but the more that heavy readers shift to subscription services, the greater the risk that publishers will see their overall revenue decline' (Thompson, 2021, 345–6). Publishers are also reluctant to lower significantly the prices of individually sold e-books outside certain genres lest this low pricing interfere with the central business model around print, impacting the price points consumers expect to pay. John Maxwell concludes that the e-book is 'marketed and sold almost exactly as if it were a paper book. It is priced lower, but often not unrecognizably lower; it is sold on a title-by-title basis, and its market performance is still reckoned in units sold, with royalties to authors still paid on more or less the same basis as print books' (Phillips and Bhaskar, 2019, 341).

In the area of audio, new business models are being found. Higher consumer revenues surround audiobooks where customers buy individual titles or join a subscription service with monthly credits, such as from Audible. Could in the future a streaming model, already used by Storytel in some markets, break open the market further by offering unlimited listening for a monthly subscription? In Europe and the USA, users know this model from Netflix and Spotify. The latter player is eyeing up the audiobook market and the partnership announced in 2021 between Storytel and Spotify could be an important game changer for the entire global audio market. In markets such as China there is considerable interest and in 2021 Tencent Music acquired the audio platform Lazy Audio, 'a comprehensive audio platform providing entertainment in the forms of audiobooks, Chinese comedy, podcasts and other radio shows to customers. It monetizes via different channels, including pay per title, subscription payment for content, and advertising' (PRNewswire, 15 January 2021). Due to constraints around market size, it is less likely that such developments will take place in smaller countries.

In the area of podcasts, revenues are derived from advertising, sponsorship, and donations; podcasts also drive other business models. Podcasters might, for example, broadcast at live events which customers pay to attend. Adding podcasts has helped to generate subscribers for music-streaming services such as Spotify. In 2020 a quarter of Spotify's monthly active users listened to podcasts, with listening hours (admittedly during a pandemic) approaching double the total in the previous year. The rising interest prompted a survey by the company to find out if users would pay for a separate podcast subscription (Perez, 2021). In the area of fiction podcasts, the model is still evolving and 'making a profit is often down to selling the story and seeing it transformed into TV, films or even novels' (Damon, 2021). Meanwhile 'Hollywood has figured out that fiction podcasts can serve as a form of cheap proof of concept, bypassing an expensive pilot that may never be greenlit' (Damon, 2021).

Experimentation continues around business models for books, including the arrival of crowdfunding for new projects. Streaming services for e-books and audio disrupt the traditional book business model and offer the membership/subscription model of a commercial circulating library. The system moves away from product to service, from what is bought to what is consumed. Payments to publishers and authors then depend on usage, with a share of the pooled income from subscribers divided up according to listening time. If an individual consumer listens to only part of an audiobook, this leads to lower income compared to the purchase of the title. The dynamic of the storytelling is to keep readers hooked and ready for the next part. This favours books that meet this requirement, whether within a single text or as part of a series that readers can follow sequentially. All-you-can-eat models of subscription bring books into line with other service models such as the streaming of music and TV but undermine the print-based business model and underline the growing separation between the digital and print worlds. The traditional definition of the (vanilla) e-book or audiobook refers to the parentage of a print edition – this is changing with digital and audio-first projects. The often serial aspects hark back to the Victorian era of fiction published in instalments. In the face of much experimentation around formats and approaches, the book business continues to operate within frameworks that are familiar, often with a long history. Yet the growth of online bookselling and streaming services offers greater knowledge about book consumers and their behaviour – such knowledge is an important game changer for how publishing develops.

Conclusion

We have presented in this volume the argument for a tripartite model of the book that operates across its information architecture, its position as a carrier for the communication of knowledge and information, and a distinct business model. The vanilla versions of the e-book and audiobook operate within the same information architecture as the print volume, often within the same copy sale business model. The colouring book is something of an outlier since no reading is involved. Focus on the book business model allows us to separate out books from products such as magazines and academic journals and to conclude that fiction online is not a book. Similarly audio-first productions and podcasts are not books, operating with a different information architecture, although they may migrate to publication in book form.

Is This a Book?

The present volume meets our technical definition of a book: it has a minimum length, an emphasis on textual content, and boundaries to its form. The work is presented within the information architecture of the book, with page numbers, chapters, a title page, and a contents list. The digital version of the book matches the print version in terms of its architecture and can be regarded as a vanilla e-book corresponding with the print version (with the exception of the dynamic Figure 3, which cannot be reproduced in the print edition). No audio version is planned but it would again most likely be a vanilla audiobook simply reproducing the text without any sophisticated theatrical production. Increasingly scholarly books such as this one adopt some of the information architecture of the journal article with an abstract and key words, whether by volume or chapter. This enables discoverability through searches of online databases (where content is available through a different business model from that of the book), and this volume will join the Cambridge Core online platform.

The authors have already co-authored two journal articles on this topic and could have continued the thread of argument with further papers in a serial publication. Yet it seemed appropriate given the subject matter to move our discussion to a book. Writing this book as a series of blog posts or as a newsletter would have been a possibility. The text would be readily accessible and could have been displayed as a series of chapters. This would offer a level of interaction with readers and the possibility of revising the text or offering additional thoughts. But it would not offer the validation of publication as part of a respected book list.

Self-publishing a book through a platform such as Amazon is an option. Many (vanilla) e-books mirror the architecture of printed works and so meet that requirement for a book. This would have been less satisfying, however, as we like to publish in print, and we would not have benefitted from the added value offered by our publisher as part of the mainstream business model, from the selection and authority of the publisher's imprint to professional editing, peer reviewing, and the circulation of the metadata through the book supply chain. The book is published by a reputable publisher that pushes high-quality metadata about the book – key information including the price, contents, and cover – into the supply chain for books. This again aids discoverability by potential readers, whether browsing the web pages of their university library, searching for relevant terms on Google, or browsing one of the major online bookstores. Publication of this text as a book puts us at the very heart of the Order of the Book.

The Dynamics of the Three-Body Model

There are three elements to the three-body model of the book: an information architecture represented most closely in the physical book but also apparent in the vanilla e-book and audiobook; the book's position within the Order of the Book as a carrier for the communication of knowledge and information; and the business model of the book which offers boundaries largely set by the economics of the printing press. The beauty of the three-body model of the book is that it opens a door to understanding the power relations that have shaped the Order of the Book in the past few centuries. Also the third element of the book is sometimes obscured by the perspective of the second, as Nicholas

Thoburn comments: 'we tend not to think of the capitalist form of books. We imagine books to be transcendent intellectual, moral and aesthetic goods unsullied by commerce, just as we perceive our own individual encounters with these quintessential objects of culture to confirm and augment only our intellect, taste, or political commitments, the textual object greeting and flattering its reading subject as if the two meet outside social determination' (Thoburn, 2016, x).

The three elements interact with each other in an open, dynamic system, just as in the Three-Body Problem in physics. Information architecture based on identicalness of the page gave birth to the protocols of the Order of the Book that shape how we produce and reproduce knowledge. Part of the protocols is, for instance, the lack of advertising that contributes to the information architecture of the book. In return the information architecture (e.g. clear, explanatory title; list of contents) feeds into the metadata that help to drive sales. The market helps to determine the information architecture of different categories of books. Children's picture books, for example, are short and keenly priced, and if text is included this may need to work for the coedition market (selling editions in other languages) with the right length of sentences and captions.

The dynamic interaction of the three elements gave birth to a set of different manifestations of the book. These manifestations – varying from hardback and paperback editions, to vanilla audio and e-books, to silent and colouring books – should not be compared with other textual media such as cuneiform born in times and places where there was no Order of the Book. Neither should the term 'book' be used for textual content that has no book information architecture and is not distributed by the book business model – such as blog posts or daily papers.

The motion of the three elements that form the book has become especially dynamic in the past three decades. The Internet has encouraged experimentation around the form of the book, aiming to move it away from a linear structure. Yet the book gave up the opportunity to become that one, great hyperlinked resource envisioned by Kevin Kelly (or Douglas Adams), and web content is different in terms of

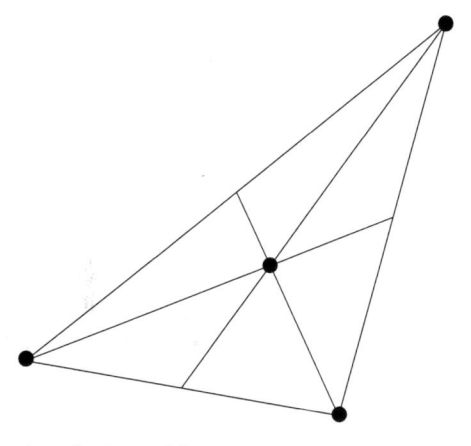

Figure 3 The three-body model
Note: an animated version of the figure is available in the online resources
(www.cambridge.org/isthisabook).
Source: Dnttllthmmnm, CC BY-SA 4.0, via Wikimedia Commons

information architecture and business model. The book remains a long-form, linear narrative with set boundaries.

If non-linear forms of text could so easily accomplish what the book format accomplishes, such as in the transmission of knowledge and culture, the book as we know it would exist only in museums alongside cuneiforms and wampum colliers. The resilience and continued appeal of print books can be explained if we consider books not as an adversary to screens or as a relic of history, but as a long-form, linear reading complement to digital reading and browsing. The book is not only a welcome refuge from the work environment of screens and a detox from our skimming habit, but also a tool that helps to boost our cognitive abilities, such as depth and breadth of vocabulary and sustained attention – valuable by-products of deep reading. A reason for the success of the vanilla e-book and dedicated reading devices is perhaps that most book readers prefer to follow linear narratives and do not wish to be distracted by hyperlinks to outside the book. The e-book format echoes the linear structure of the printed book and its information architecture; however, this echo is not yet strong enough for the e-book to outperform the print book and its perceived benefits.

Because of the enduring market demand for long-form reading, the information architecture of the book has proved to be resilient in the face of glitzy new possibilities whether in gaming or in the arena of social media. The appeal of the book remains that it is self-contained, non-porous, static with boundaries. Book authors are rarely keen to update their works every five minutes, and most prefer the book's linear narrative structure. In turn readers still want something apart from the Internet that is fixed and internally coherent – they want to read text that has been reworked a number of times to achieve something that is considered and well structured.

Book reading helps to build empathy whilst developing literacy, critical thinking, and the knowledge society that are seen as core benefits in societies interwoven by the protocols of the Order of the Book – hence the book is part of a special regime that often includes lower taxation as well as subsidies for actors in the value chain, from publishers and booksellers to libraries. The tax advantages contribute to the workings of the business model. In turn other products with book information architecture such as colouring books and diaries are attracted into the business model although they may not truly belong there.

Understanding what a book is allows further analysis of its role and future. What is the place of reading and books in the digital landscape? Intriguingly our quick-fire reading habits on the Web open up a clear space for long-form, immersive reading. Reading fiction enables us to enter other worlds and other minds and to immerse ourselves in stories fuelled by the writer's imagination. Serious non-fiction asks us to grapple with ideas, events, and stories of interesting lives. For example, as suggested by Stuart Ritchie, popular science books can 'translate complex scientific results for the general reader in ways that neither exaggerate nor distort, providing new means how to think about ourselves and the world' (2020, 152). Reading develops in us a whole set of critical faculties, and Dan Visel comments that 'it is not the form of the book that is most worth protecting. Rather, it is what the image of the book stands for, a vehicle for the transfer of big ideas and experiences. Any number of new forms can potentially accomplish this. But it's the already literate who are in a position to best take advantage of this: to analyse the bias of a post on Facebook without thinking about it, to find symbolism in the television drama of the week' (2014, 15).

Is the Order of the Book still alive and kicking, or is it slowly dissolving, moving the book to a less prominent position in the media hierarchy? In this book, we have given more than a few hints that the latter might indeed be the case. There is no question that the book's role in the dissemination of knowledge and information has diminished. If whole categories of knowledge continue their move on to the Internet, acquiring new, unprecedented formats, what is left for the printed book? Is it the home of critical thinking – through deep, long-form reading? Is it perhaps story? – either fiction or narrative non-fiction such as memoir or biography. Are books now just one of many forms of adaptation of story, part of a transmedia journey? For example, from book to audio, screen, or game; or in the other direction from game to book, from screen to book, from web or social media to streaming to book? A good example is Douglas Adams and *The Hitchhiker's Guide to Galaxy* way back in the 1980s. Many new works of fiction are readily available on literature and fan fiction websites, and successful ones attract a lot of attention and many readers. There are many different forms of story-telling that the contemporary author can pursue, whether a Netflix series or a podcast, as described by the UK literary agent Jonny Geller from Curtis Brown: 'we can now have a storyteller tell a story and I can think well actually this would work better as a ten part series and then the book' (Phillips, 2020, 174).

The dynamics of the tripartite model suggest that the risks for the book can come from multiple directions. Already the unit of currency in many academic disciplines is the journal article, not the book. The merging of the information architecture of book and journal, apparent in many library databases (and this book will join an online database), disguises the origin of book content and blur boundaries. The collapse of the traditional business model in some book sectors, whether through the availability of free content on the Web or the adoption of a service model for digital access, has lessened the book's role in the supply of information and its role in education. Print runs in many countries are still supported by purchasing from the public library network, but there is an uncertain future for libraries in some countries, often the victim of budget cuts. Governments seduced by digital access and ignorant of the benefits of deep, long-form reading will increasingly question the role of the book in education, or in society more broadly, in the communication of knowledge and information.

The opportunities from streaming models for e-books and audio are clear; so too are the risks for industry and author revenues from consumer publishing. Yet publishers run the risk of being left behind if the streaming services come to generate much of their own content. The Internet has disrupted retail as well as the supply of content. In some countries physical bookstores are supported by grants for smaller shops and by a system of controlled pricing. For how long will such policies be seen as justifiable? In many markets the shift towards online purchasing is a notable trend (accelerated by the pandemic) and physical bookstores often keep going only by selling a broader range of stock including gifts and stationery. For books the Internet works well if you know what you want or are happy to be guided by algorithms – but how do you discover *The Hitchhiker's Guide to the Galaxy* when visiting from another country? Often the delights of serendipity come from a visit to a physical store, as Mark Forsyth recalls:

> I never had any desire to read Ukrainian crime-comedy until 2001. I was promenading around a bookshop in north London and I saw a book called *Death and the Penguin*. It was out on a table, not the first table when you come in the door (footballers' autobiographies), but the table a little way back where the good stuff is always hidden. I liked the title – the move from abstract noun to concrete – I liked the cover – a man with a gun sitting in

a bath with a huge penguin . . . There are times when you
can't part with your money quick enough. (2014, 9)

How do we answer the question as to whether the book still matters?
By reminding ourselves of the value of books in terms of the pleasure
they give and their ability to stimulate thinking through deep reading.
To the surprise of many the book is still hanging on in there: Laura
Miller tells us that we live in 'an era of intense fascination with the very
concept of information – how to acquire it, own it, and deploy it for
personal gain and public welfare. This respect for discrete information
joins with an older regard for education and, at least for some, real
pleasure to be gained from the act of reading. In each of these areas,
books – and bookstores – still play an important mediating function'
(Miller, 2011, 24).

We must preach the value of whole books and long-form reading.
Non-fiction offers sustained arguments and considered thought, whilst
fiction takes us to imaginary worlds and tells many of the lasting stories
that find their way into radio, TV, and film. The novelist Kazuo
Ishiguro reflects on his work: 'It is important for me this question
about writing things that linger on the mind, or linger in people's
feelings, long after the reading experience is over . . . If you are really
lucky and you have done your work really well, you'll still be there
days, months, even years later' (Ishiguro, 2021).

To maintain the book's privileges, the arguments for the value of
long-form reading need to be restated. As shown by meta-studies into
the differences between print and digital reading, print still has a place in
education at all levels, and time away from screens is beneficial for both
children and adults. The book remains the bastion of both deep and
immersive reading. The lessons around reading and learning need to be
widely disseminated. Reading is invaluable for the development of
cognitive abilities and sustained concentration. None of this is to say
that skimming should be abandoned in the name of deep reading. Just
the opposite, as skimming and deep reading are a perfect match: the
former allows us to surf seas of information and dive in where we find
something of interest; our experience of deep reading enables us to

understand more fully the complexity of social, cultural, and natural phenomena.

The challenges of the modern world leave us searching for answers to the world's problems and new ways of thinking. Books remain an invaluable tool to help us develop our analytical, abstract, and strategic thinking. Of course this may not always be the case – other tools may appear to replace this aspect of books – but in the meantime let us celebrate the power of books and the joy they bring to many.

References

Adams, T. R., and Barker, N. (1993). 'A New Model for the Study of the Book'. In *Potencie of Life: Books in the Society*. London: British Library.

Audio Publishers Association (2021). 'A First Look at Digital Audiobook Tracking', 21 January. www.audiopub.org/blog/a-first-look-at-digital-audiobook-tracking-from-the-npd-group

Barbier, F. (2001). *Histoire du livre*. Paris: Armand Colin.

Baron, N. (2015). *Words on Screen: The Fate of Reading in a Digital World*. Oxford: Oxford University Press.

Baron, N. (2021). *How We Read Now: The Fate of Reading in a Digital World*. Oxford: Oxford University Press.

Baverstock, A. Bradford, R., and Gonzalez, M., eds. (2020). *Contemporary Publishing and the Culture of Books*. Abingdon: Routledge.

BBC (2020). Douglas Stuart interviewed on the *R4 Today* programme, 20 November.

Benjamin, W. (2008). *The Work of Art in the Age of Its Technical Reproducibility and Other Writings on Media*. Cambridge, MA: The Belknap Press of Harvard University Press.

Berglund, K. and Steiner, A. (2021). 'Is Backlist the New Frontlist? Large-Scale Data Analysis of Bestseller Book Consumption in Streaming Services', *Logos*, 32:1, 7–24.

Berret, C. (2017). 'Walter Benjamin and the Question of Print in Media History', *Journal of Communication Inquiry*, 41:4, 349–67.

Bhaskar, M. (2013). *The Content Machine*. London: Anthem.

Bhaskar, M. (2016). *Curation*. London: Piatkus.

Blair, A. (2011). *Too Much to Know: Managing Scholarly Information before the Modern Age*. New Haven, CT: Yale University Press.

Bown, J. (2009). *Exposure*. London: Guardian Books.

Buchweitz, A., Mason, R. A., Tomitch, L. M. B., and Just, M. A. (2009). 'Brain Activation for Reading and Listening Comprehension: An fMRI Study of Modality Effects and Individual Differences in Language Comprehension', *Psychology & Neuroscience*, 2:2, 111–23.

Calasso, R. (2015). *The Art of the Publisher*. Farrar Straus & Giroux, New York.

Carmody, T. (2010). '10 Reading Revolutions before e-Books', *Atlantic*, 10 August.

Carroll, L. (1865). *Alice's Adventures in Wonderland*. London: Macmillan

Cavalho, G., and Chartier, R. (1999). *A History of Reading in the West*. Oxford: Blackwell.

Cernik, L. (2018). '"Worst Store" in Britain? Here's Why I Still Love WH Smith', *Guardian*, 29 May.

Chang, J., and Halliday, J. (2007). *Mao: The Unknown Story*. London: Vintage.

Clark, G., and Phillips, A. (2019). *Inside Book Publishing*, 6th edition. Abingdon: Routledge.

Clinton, V. (2019). 'Reading from Paper Compared to Screens: A Systematic Review and Meta-analysis', *Journal of Research in Reading*, 42:2, 268–87.

Daly, L. (2013). 'The Year's Best eBooks Are Games'. https://worldwritable.com/wordplay-f9fa68ae997e#.i6ii4uvid

Damon, P. (2021). 'Movies for the Ears', *Sunday Times*, 28 March.

Daniel, D. B., and Woody, W. D. (2010). 'They Hear, but Do Not Listen: Retention for Podcasted Material in a Classroom Context', *Teaching of Psychology*, 37, 199–203.

Darnton, R. (1982). 'What Is the History of Books?', *Daedalus*, 111:3, 65–83.

Delgado, P., Vargas, C., Ackerman, R., and Salmerón, L. (2018). 'Don't Throw Away Your Printed Books: A Meta-analysis on the Effects of Reading Media on Comprehension', *Educational Research Review*, 25, 23–38.

Deloitte, *Technology, Media, and Telecommunications Predictions 2020* (2019), Deloitte Insights.

Drucker, P. F. (1999). *Management Challenges for the 21st Century*. New York: Harper Business.

Edgecliffe-Johnson, A. (2019). 'Audio Gives New Voice to Books in the Digital Age', *Financial Times*, 18 December.

Edison Research (2020). *The Infinite Dial*. Edison Research and Triton Digital.

Eisenstein, E. (1980). *The Printing Press As an Agent of Change*. Cambridge: Cambridge University Press.

Eliot, S., and Rose, J. (2007). *A Companion to the History of the Book*. Oxford: Blackwell.

Feather, J. (1988). *A History of British Publishing*. London: Routledge.

Fischer, S. R. (2003). *A History of Reading*. London: Reaktion Books.

Forsyth, M. (2014). *The Unknown Unknown: Bookshops and the Delight of Not Getting What You Wanted*. London: Icon Books.

Fry, S. (2008). *The Machine That Made Us*. BBC documentary.

Furedi, F. (2015). *Power of Reading: From Socrates to Twitter*. London: Bloomsbury.

Garfinkle, A. (2021). 'The Erosion of Deep Literacy', *National Affairs*, 49, 192–208.

Genette, G. (1997). *Paratexts: Thresholds of Interpretation*. Cambridge: Cambridge University Press.

Gfk (2019). *Who Borrows What in Libraries and Especially Online? A 360 Degree Look at Germany's Digital Public Library Service 'Onleihe'*. Study based on the GfK Consumer Panel Media Scope, Boersenverein's des Deutschen Buchhandels (German Publishers and Booksellers Association), November. file:///C:/Users/p0017526/Downloads/Praesentation_Onleihe_Berlin_2019_final_ENG.pdf

Goody, J., and Watt, I. (1968). 'The Consequences of Literacy', in *Literacy in Traditional Societies*, ed. J. Goody. Cambridge: Cambridge University Press.

Gould, S. J. (1994). 'So Near and Yet so Far', *New York Review of Books*, 20 October.

Graeber, D. (2016). *The Utopia of Rules*. New York: Melville House.

Gustafsson, H. (2021). 'The Market for Audiobooks', *Logos*, 32:2, 7–9.

Have, I., and Pedersen, B. S. (2013). 'Sonic Mediatization of the Book: Affordances of the Audiobook', *MedieKultur*, 54, 123–40.

Havelock, E. A. (1986). *The Muse Learns to Write: Reflections on Orality and Literacy from Antiquity to the Present*. New Haven, CT: Yale University Press.

Heathcote, E. (2020). 'When Bookshelves Are More Informative Than the Books', *Financial Times*, 15 April.

Howard, N. (2005). *The Book: The Life Story of a Technology*. Westport, CT: Greenwood Press.

IBISWorld (2021), *Audiobook Publishing in the UK*. IBIS World.

IPA-FEP (2019). *VAT on Books*, Annual Global Report. https://international publishers.org/images/aa-content/news/news-2019/IPA_ANNUAL_GLOBAL_REPORT_2018_2.pdf

Ishiguro, K. (2021). Interviewed by Krishnan Guru-Murthy, Ways to Change the World podcast, 5 March. www.channel4.com/news/ways-to-change-the-world

Jaynes, J. (2000). *The Origin of Consciousness in the Breakdown of the Bicameral Mind*. New York: Houghton Mifflin.

Johns, A. (1998). *The Nature of the Book: Print and Knowledge in the Making*. Chicago: University of Chicago Press.

Johnson, M. (2021). *Books and Social Media: How the Digital Age Is Shaping the Printed Word*. Abingdon: Routledge.

Johnston, C., ed. (2019). *The Concept of the Book*. London: Institute of English Studies.

Jones, N. (2020). 'The Fourth Format', in Baverstock, Bradford, and Gonzalez, *Contemporary Publishing and the Culture of Books*.

Kapr, A. (1996). *Johann Gutenberg: The Man and His Invention*. Abingdon: Routledge.

Kelly, K. (2006). 'Scan this Book!', *New York Times*, 14 May.

Kershaw, I. (2010). *Hitler*. London: Penguin.

Kintsch, W., and Kozminsky, E. (1977). 'Summarizing Stories after Reading and Listening', *Journal of Educational Psychology*, 69:5, 491–9.

Klose, S., and Puckett, J. (2017). 'Audio in Stereo', *Library Journal*, November, 28–32.

Kobo (2016). *How the Best Readers in the World Read*, April. https://news.objects.frb.io/assets/159/files/20163/Kobo+Data+White paper+-+APRIL_2016.pdf

Kovač, M. (2008). *Never Mind the Web: Here Comes the Book*. Oxford: Chandos.

Kovač, M. (2015). 'Bokes be not set by, there times is past, I gesse: Reflections on the End of the Book', *Logos*, 26:4, 7–21.

Kovač, M., Phillips, A., van der Weel, A., and Wischenbart, R. (2017). 'Book Statistics: What Are They Good For?', *Logos*, 28:4, 7–17.

Kovač, M., Phillips, A., van der Weel, A., and Wischenbart, R. (2019). 'What Is a Book?', *Publishing Research Quarterly*, 35:3, 313–26.

Kovač, M., and van der Weel, A. (2018). 'Reading in a Post-textual Era', *First Monday*, 23:10.

Kovač, M., and Wischenbart, R. (2019). 'Globalization and Publishing', in Phillips and Bhaskar, *Oxford Handbook of Publishing*.

Kozloff, S. (1995). 'Audio Books in a Visual Culture', *Journal of American Culture*, 18:4, 83–95.

Krummel, D. W. (2013). 'The Heritage of Boleslas Iwinski', *Library Trends* 62:2, 456–64.

References

Kulundžić, Z. (1959). *Put do Knjige*. Zagreb: Epoha.

Lennon, R. (2020). Publishing Director at Penguin Random House Audio, interviewed by Angus Phillips, 16 November. https://oxfordpublish.org/podcasts/item/angus_phillips_in_conversation_with_richard_lennon

Liu, Z. (2005). 'Reading Behavior in the Digital Environment: Changes in Reading Behavior over the Past Ten Years', *Journal of Documentation*, 61:6, 700–12.

Lyons, M. (2010). *A History of Reading and Writing in the Western World*. London: Palgrave Macmillan.

Lyons, M. (2011). *Books: A Living History*. London: Thames and Hudson.

Marchetti, E., and Valente, A. (2018). 'Interactivity and Multimodality in Language Learning: The Untapped Potential of Audiobooks', *Universal Access in the Information Society*, 17:2, 257–74.

Maughan, S. (2017). 'Riding the Growth in Audio', *Publishers Weekly*, 6 November, 6–10.

Miller, L. (2011). 'Perpetual Turmoil: Book Retailing in the Twenty-First Century United States', *Logos*, 22:3, 16–25.

Mod, C. (2019). *Ridgeline*, issue 30, July. https://craigmod.com/ridgeline/030

Murray, A. (2020). 'Padraig Harrington Launched a YouTube Channel for Club Golfers, *Guardian*, 6 November.

Murray, S. (2018). *The Digital Literary Sphere: Reading, Writing and Selling Books in the Internet Era*. Baltimore, MD: Johns Hopkins University Press.

Murray, S. (2020). *Introduction to Contemporary Print Culture: Books As Media*. Abingdon: Routledge.

Michael, E. B., Keller, T. A., Carpenter, P. A., and Just, M. A. (2001). 'fMRI Investigation of Sentence Comprehension by Eye and by Ear: Modality Fingerprints on Cognitive Processes', *Human Brain Mapping*, 13:4, 239–52.

Nielsen Book Research (2020). *Understanding the UK Audiobook Consumer 2020*.

O'Leary, B. (2010). 'A Unified Field Theory of Publishing', Books in Browsers Conference, 21 October. https://magellanmediapartners .com/publishing-innovation/a-unified-field-theory-of-publishing

Ong, W. J. (1982). *Orality and Literacy: The Technologizing of the Word*. New York: Methuen.

Osterwalder, A., and Pigneur, Y. (2010). *Business Model Generation*. Hoboken, NJ: Wiley.

Perez, S. (2021). 'Spotify Plans for Podcast Subscriptions, à la carte Payments'. 3 February. https://techcrunch.com

Pew Research (2019). 'One-in-Five Americans Now Listen to Audiobooks', 25 September. www.pewresearch.org/fact-tank/2019/ 09/25/one-in-five-americans-now-listen-to-audiobooks

Phillips, A. (2014). *Turning the Page*. Abingdon: Routledge.

Phillips, A. (2020). 'The Modern Literary Agent', in Baverstock, Bradford, and Gonzalez (2020).

Phillips, A., and Bhaskar, M., ed. (2019). *The Oxford Handbook of Publishing*. Oxford: Oxford University Press.

Phillips. A., and Cope, B., eds. (2006). *The Future of the Book in the Digital Age*. Oxford: Chandos.

Podcast Insights (2021). *Podcast Stats and Facts*. www.podcastinsights .com/podcast-statistics

Pressman, J. (2021). *Bookishness: Loving Books in a Digital Age*. New York: Columbia University Press.

Price, L. (2012). 'Dead Again', *New York Times Book Review*, 12 August.

Price, L. (2019). *What We Talk about When We Talk about Books*. London: Basic Books.

PRNewswire (2021). 'China Literature Announces Sale of Lazy Audio'. www.prnewswire.com/news-releases/china-literature-announces-sale-of-its-equity-interest-in-lazy-audio-for-rmb1-08-billion-3

Raine, C. (1979). *A Martian Sends a Postcard Home*. Oxford: Oxford University Press.

Raphel, A. (2015). 'Why Adults Are Buying Coloring Books (for Themselves)', *New Yorker*, 12 July.

Raven, J. (2019). *What Is the History of the Book?* Cambridge: Polity.

Raven, J., ed. (2020). *The Oxford Illustrated History of the Book*. Oxford: Oxford University Press.

Ritchie, S. (2020). *Science Fictions: Exposing Fraud, Bias, Negligence and Hype in Science*. London: Bodley Head.

Ronning, H., and Slaatta, T. (2019). *The Tools of Literary Politics. The Norwegian Model*. Oslo: Scandinavian Academic Press and Spartacus Forlag.

Ronning, H., and Slaatta, T. (2020). *Ambitious Literary Policies: International Perspectives*. Oslo and Geneva: Norwegian Publishers Association and International Publishers Association.

Rose, J. (2010). *The Intellectual Life of the British Working Classes*, 2nd edition. New Haven, CT: Yale University Press.

Roupenian, K. (2017). 'Cat Person', *New Yorker*, 4 September.

Rubery, M. (2016). *The Untold Story of the Talking Book*. Cambridge, MA: Harvard University Press.

Schofield, J. (1994). 'Books Enter a New Chapter', *Guardian*, 24 March.

Schofield, J. (2009). 'Amazon Caves to Authors Guild over Kindle's Text-to-Speech Reading', *Guardian*, 1 March.

Sebag Montefiore, S. (2003). *Stalin: The Court of the Red Tsar*. London: Weidenfeld & Nicolson.

Singer, L. M., and Alexander, P. A. (2017). 'Reading on Paper and Digitally: What the Past Decades of Empirical Research Reveal', *Review of Educational Research*, 87:6, 1007–41.

Sousa, T. L. V., Carriere, J. S. A., and Smilek, D. (2013). 'The Way We Encounter Reading Material Influences How Frequently We Mind Wander', *Frontiers in Psychology*, 28 November.

Suarez, M., and Woudhuysen, H. R. (2010). *The Oxford Companion to the Book*. Oxford: Oxford University Press.

Suarez, M., and Woudhuysen, H. R. (2013). *The Book: A Global History*. Oxford: Oxford University Press.

Thoburn, N. (2016). *Anti-book: On the Art and Politics of Radical Publishing*. Minneapolis: University of Minnesota Press.

Thompson, J. (2005). *Books in the Digital Age*. Cambridge: Polity Press.

Thompson, J. (2021). *Book Wars: The Digital Revolution in Publishing*. Cambridge: Polity Press.

Towheed, S., Crone, R., and Halsey, K. (2011). *The History of Reading: A Reader*. Abingdon: Routledge.

Trump, M. L. (2020). *Too Much and Never Enough: How My Family Created the World's Most Dangerous Man*. London: Simon and Schuster.

Vaidhyanathan, S. (2018). *Antisocial Media*. New York: Oxford University Press.

van der Weel, A. (2010). 'e-Roads and i-Ways: A Sociotechnical Look at User Acceptance of e-Books', *Logos*, 21:3–4, 47–57.

van der Weel, A. (2011). *Changing Our Textual Minds: Towards a Digital Order of Knowledge*. Manchester: Manchester University Press.

van der Weel, A. (2014). 'From an Ownership to an Access Economy of Publishing', *Logos*, 25:2, 39–46.

Visel, D. (2014). 'The Book and Place, the Place of the Book', in *Exploring the Boundaries of the Book*, ed. M. Spruit. Leiden: TXT.

Warkentin, G. (1999). 'In Search of "The World of the Other": Aboriginal Sign Systems and the History of the Book in Canada', *Book History*, 2, 1–27.

Weber, M. (1905). *The Protestant Ethic and the Spirit of Capitalism*. 2001 edition. Abingdon: Routledge.

Weedon, A. (2010). Preface to Robinson, P., and Roberts, R., *The History of the Book in the West: 400AD–1455*. Farnham: Ashgate.

Willingham, D. T. (2017). *The Reading Mind: A Cognitive Approach to Understanding How the Mind Reads*. New York: Wiley.

Wischenbart, R. (2008). 'Ripping off the Cover: Has Digitization Changed What's Really in the book?', *Logos*, 19:4, 196–202.

Wolf, M. (2018). *Reader, Come Home: The Reading Brain in a Digital World*. New York: Harper, 2018.

Wolf, M. and Barzillai, M. (2009). 'The Importance of Deep Reading', *Literacy 2.0*, 66:6, 32–7.

Wolfson, G. (2008). 'Using Audiobooks to Meet the Needs of Adolescent Readers', *American Secondary Education*, 36:2, 105–14.

Zaid, G. (2004). *So Many Books*. London: Sort of Books.

Acknowledgements

This book has its origins in two papers co-authored with Adriaan van der Weel and Rüdiger Wischenbart, and we would like to express our thanks to them for their co-operation and good will. Discussion around the topic of 'what is a book?' occurred at meetings of the E-READ COST network and at the By the Book conference in Florence. To our colleagues from around Europe, including members of the Zadar Swimming Club, we express our gratitude for many fruitful debates.

We are grateful to Adriaan van der Weel, Michael Bhaskar, Jaka Gerčar, and the anonymous reviewers who read a draft of the text and contributed useful feedback.

Angus would like to thank colleagues at the Oxford International Centre for Publishing for their support and good humour. Also his family – Ann, Matthew, Charlotte, and Jamie – who continue to cheer on his writing.

Miha would like to thank colleagues in Ljubljana who helped him with his book on reading (published in Slovene), work on which contributed to the reading chapter in this Element. He is more than grateful to his family for their patience – he becomes quite an unbearable person when he switches to writing mode.

About the Authors

Angus Phillips is Professor of Publishing and Director of the Oxford International Centre for Publishing at Oxford Brookes University. He has degrees from Oxford and Warwick universities and before joining Oxford Brookes he ran a trade and reference list at Oxford University Press. His previous books include *Turning the Page* and *Inside Book Publishing* (with Giles Clark). He is the co-editor (with Michael Bhaskar) of *The Oxford Handbook of Publishing* and the chief editor of the premier publishing journal *Logos*. His books have been translated into seven languages.

Miha Kovač is Professor of Publishing Studies at the University of Ljubljana. Before joining academia, he worked as an editorial director in the two largest Slovenian publishing houses, DZS and Mladinska knjiga, and as editorial director of the Slovenian edition of *National Geographic* magazine. His previous academic book, written in English, is *Never Mind the Web*. His latest book *Read to Breathe* (written and first published in Slovenian) is being translated into six languages.

Cambridge Elements ☰

Publishing and Book Culture

SERIES EDITOR

Samantha Rayner
University College London

Samantha Rayner is Professor of Publishing and Book
Cultures at UCL. She is also Director of UCL's Centre for
Publishing, co-Director of the Bloomsbury CHAPTER
(Communication History, Authorship, Publishing, Textual
Editing and Reading) and co-Chair of the Bookselling
Research Network.

ASSOCIATE EDITOR

Leah Tether
University of Bristol

Leah Tether is Professor of Medieval Literature and Publishing
at the University of Bristol. With an academic background in
medieval French and English literature and a professional
background in trade publishing, Leah has combined her
expertise and developed an international research profile in
book and publishing history from manuscript to digital.

About the Series

This series aims to fill the demand for easily accessible, quality texts available for teaching and research in the diverse and dynamic fields of Publishing and Book Culture. Rigorously researched and peer-reviewed Elements will be published under themes, or 'Gatherings'. These Elements should be the first check point for researchers or students working on that area of publishing and book trade history and practice: we hope that, situated so logically at Cambridge University Press, where academic publishing in the UK began, it will develop to create an unrivalled space where these histories and practices can be investigated and preserved.

Cambridge Elements ≡

Publishing and Book Culture

THE BUSINESS OF PUBLISHING

Gathering Editor: Rachel Noorda

Dr. Rachel Noorda is the Director of Publishing at Portland State University. Dr. Noorda is a researcher of twenty-first-century book studies, particularly on topics of entrepreneurship, marketing, small business, national identity, and international publishing.

ELEMENTS IN THE SERIES

Entrepreneurial Identity in US Book Publishing in the Twenty-First Century
Rachel Noorda

Is This a Book?
Angus Phillips and Miha Kovač

A full series listing is available at: www.cambridge.org/EPBC

Printed in the United States
by Baker & Taylor Publisher Services